Did I Win?

A FAREWELL TO
GEORGE SHEEHAN

DID I
WIN?

BY HIS FRIEND
JOE HENDERSON

WRS
PUBLISHING

A Division of WRS Group, Inc.
Waco, Texas

First published in the United States of America in 1995 by WRS Publishing,
A division of WRS Group, Inc., 701 N. New Road, Waco, Texas 76710
Book design by Colleen Robishaw
Jacket design by Joe James

10 9 8 7 6 5 4 3 2

Library of Congress Cataloging-in-Publication Data

Henderson, Joe, 1943–
         Did I Win? : a farewell to George Sheehan / by his friend Joe
Henderson.
                    p.   cm.

         1. Sheehan, George. 2 Runners (Sports—United States—
Biography. 3. Sportswriters—United States—Biography. 4.
Physicians—United States—Biography. 5. Runner's world.
         I. Title.
GV1016.15.S47H46   1995
796.4'2'092—dc20
[B]
                                                          94-31756
                                                          CIP
ISBN 1-56796-066-9
ISBN 1-56796-106-1 pbk.

DEDICATION

To runners everywhere:
George Sheehan loved you
for letting him be who he was
and do all he did.

CONTENTS

RIGHT CHOICES

BY GEORGE SHEEHAN III

I am Dr. George Sheehan's oldest son. Nearly twenty years ago, when my physician father decided to devote more time to his writing and speaking pursuits, he hired me as his business manager. This later became a full-time job.

You would think that being so close to Dad, and a runner as well, I would know him like a book and would never be stumped by the challenge of a True Believer: "You know what your father says about that, don't you?" But quite often, I am stumped.

Many people can quote Dad better than I. One reason for this may be surprising: I rarely took the time to read his books.

Working at the office, however, allowed me to see the material in advance. It would first appear in print in his weekly newspaper column. His books, in effect, were quilt-like selections of those columns. They were culled and stitched into thematic chapters.

I think it was that selection and arrangement which made his ideas so memorable. Few people know this editing was, in all but one of those books, the work of Joe Henderson.

Dad and Joe first met in 1968 at the Mexico City Olympics. Dad was there to experience the Games, then write a report for his local newspaper. Joe was covering the Games for *Track & Field News*. The two became *simpatico*. In 1970, Joe asked Dad to write for *Runner's World*. Thus began their professional relationship that lasted the rest of Dad's life.

Both quickly became part of the vanguard of the running boom. Joe shared his deep knowledge of the history and technique of the sport. He changed the face of road-running training (and gave new meaning to the term "LSD") with his book on long slow distance.

Dad first focussed his thoughts on medical advance but then went on to examine the deeper philosophical question: Why were people turning to this lonely world of distance running?

They both struck a chord. Joe was not only receiving and processing all of Dad's writing, but they both were in demand on the lecture circuit, where their paths crossed often.

No one in the running community was as close to Dad as Joe Henderson. No one is better able to tell the George Sheehan story. Indeed in Dad's last weeks, as he struggled to finish his own final book, I came across some scribbled notes among his writing. "Who will finish the book if I go?" the first sentence read. The next line was, "Maybe Joe?"

This trust in Joe has to do with Dad's notion of "class." For Dad, having class means making the right choices. In his view, Joe is such a person. In this wonderful book, Joe has done it again. He has chosen writings, interviews, personal stories, tributes from friends and family, and stitched them into a beautiful quilt. *Did I Win?* gives the reader a total picture of a private man. For me, reading it has brought Dad back to life.

How would Dad react to all this? Somehow I see him as he usually was after races, standing near the finish chute, waving his fist in the air as people came across the line.

"Attaboy, Joe, baby!" he yells. "Hey, way to go!"

To which I add, "Amen."

WINNING WAYS

Six years into his struggle with the disease that would take his life in 1993, George Sheehan wrote a column about a speech he'd just given in San Diego. "I was standing on the altar of a Unitarian Church, answering questions from the runners in front of me."

The nature of their questions surprised George—a bestselling author, *Runner's World* magazine's favorite columnist and the most eloquent voice in his sport. These runners weren't asking him how to run a faster 10K, how to carbohydrate-load or how to treat tendinitis. The questions went deeper. "What would you do differently if you could?" someone asked. "Have you become more religious?" another listener wanted to know. A third wondered, "What are your main concerns?"

George tackled only the last of those questions, and then only in the singular—his one main concern. "I was silent for a time," he wrote. "Then with my arms in front of me, palms upward as if in supplication, I looked heavenward and asked, 'Did I win?'"

This question might well have been the guideline or trademark of George's remarkable life. "Did I Win?" might now stand as his most fitting epitath. "Although I am seventy-something," he explained in that column, "I still wonder whether I played this game of life well enough to win. It is so difficult to know what really mattered. It's as if all my life was spent studying for a final examination, and now I am not sure just what was important and what wasn't.

"Did I win? Does any one of us know? Is there anything we have done which assures us we have passed the test? Can we be sure we did our best at whatever it was that we were supposed to do?"

George often referred to himself as an "experiment of one," an ongoing study in which he was both observer and subject. No one else could determine the outcome for him. "Experiment" is another name for "test," which is a shorter version of "contest," which is a a word for "game" or "race." George was always competing—with fellow experimenters, yes, but mainly with that toughest of all competitors: himself.

"Not to yield says it all," he wrote in his bestselling book, *Running & Being*. "The enduring, the surviving does not stop with age. We may even grow more skillful at it as the years pass."

In the book, *This Running Life*, he added, "I will not last forever. But I am damn well going to know I have been here." And later in that same book: "There is nothing more certain than the defeat of a man who gives up. And, I might add, the victory of one who will not."

These lines took on new meaning when he learned in 1986 that he had a terminal illness. He fought it to the finish, which he didn't reach until almost eight years after the diagnosis. He ran scores of races, wrote dozens of columns, gave countless speeches, and completed three books in those years.

He kept experimenting, testing, competing, performing to the end. I had a front-row seat for many of George Sheehan's finest performances.

Our connection spanned the entire twenty-five years of his writing career, from his first newspaper column (written about the 1968 Olympics) to his last book (finished within days of death). I recruited him to write his long-running column for *Runner's World* (for no pay at first) and assisted on all but one of his eight books (the one that sold best). We talked by phone a hundred times a year and traded an equal number of letters.

George was my best friend in this business and passion that we shared. On a shelf above my desk sits a photo of him running that still looks down and inspires me when the words are slow to come. It's captioned with one of his own lines: "Winning is never having to say I quit."

Did he win? You be the judge after reading his story that begins with our first meeting.

ACKNOWLEDGMENTS

I wrote many books before this one. Some have been collaborations with one or two coauthors, but none so much a team effort as this book. The outpouring of affection for George Sheehan and cooperation in telling his story was so great that I feel less like an author than a master of ceremonies, introducing the many storytellers.

Dr. Wayman Spence gave us this forum. He called soon after George's death, suggesting that his company publish a tribute to our friend. We thank our teammates:

Mary Jane Sheehan for giving the family's blessing to this project, and for opening her photo album and trusting us with the only copies of these treasures.

George Sheehan III for granting blanket permission to quote from his father's writing, and for acting as what he called "the department of corrections" on the manuscript.

George Hirsch and Amby Burfoot for sharing pieces published in *Runner's World*, and Cristina Negron for editing George Sheehan's final columns in that magazine.

The essayists, who wrote sidebars to the chapters, for working without pay so their fees could go into a memorial fund. (Each is credited separately with his or her essay.)

John Brant and Robert Cullinane for supplying material beyond what appears in their essays.

Asbury Park Press and *Red Bank Register* for originally publishing George's columns and for keeping him writing regularly all those years.

Joe Fox, an editor at Random House, for allowing us to excerpt from Jim Fixx's *Complete Book of Running*.

Tim McLoone for organizing and emceeing the tribute dinner to George that we refer to often here.

Steve Toon, the WRS Publishing editor, for bringing the book into print on schedule under the tightest of deadlines.

Barbara Shaw, my wife, for understanding this was a long goodbye to George that I had to say.

PART I

CHANGES OF LIFE

(1918-1985)

GEORGE SHEEHAN TIMELINE:

1918	Born November 5 in Brooklyn, New York, as first of George and Loretta Ennis Sheehan's 14 children
1939	Runs 4:19 mile when record is 4:06
1940	Graduates from Manhattan College and stops running
1943	Earns medical degree from Long Island College of Medicine
1943–46	Serves in U.S. Navy, including duty in South Pacific
1944	Marries Mary Jane Fleming
1944	First of 12 children born (twins George and Mary Jane)
1947	Son Timothy born
1948	Daughter Ann born
1949	Opens cardiology practice in Red Bank, New Jersey
1949	Daughter Nora born
1953	Daughter Sarah born
1954	Son Peter born
1955	Son Andrew born
1957	Son John born
1958	Son Stephen born
1959	Helps found Christian Brothers Academy in Lincroft, New Jersey

1960	Daughter Monica born
1961	Son Michael born
1963	Returns to running and racing
1964	Runs his first Boston Marathon
1968	Begins writing career by covering Mexico City Olympics, which leads to a regular column in the Red Bank Register
1969	Runs 4:47 mile, world's first sub-five-minute time by a 50-year-old
1970	Writes first column for *Runner's World* magazine
1972	Publishes first book, the *Encyclopedia of Athletic Medicine*
1974	Gives first major lecture to a sports-podiatry group in San Francisco
1975	Publishes *Dr. Sheehan on Running* book
1978	Publishes *Running & Being,* which spends 14 weeks on the *New York Times* bestseller list
1978	Publishes *Medical Advice for Runners* book
1979	Runs his fastest Boston Marathon, 3:01 at age 60
1980	Publishes *This Running Life* book
1981	Receives special "Lifelong Commitment" award from President's Council on Physical Fitness and Sports
1982	Moves his column from *Runner's World* to *The Runner* magazine
1983	Publishes *How to Feel Great 24 Hours a Day* book
1984	Runs 21st consecutive, and last, Boston Marathon
1984	Tests negative for suspected prostate cancer after a growth discovered in routine exam

C H A P T E R   1

FIRST MEETING

I met Dr. George Sheehan where neither of us should have been that morning. From different directions, he from the East Coast and I from the West, we had come to this Olympic city. Now, together, we were about to break into the Olympic Village.

This wasn't the real village, where the athletes stayed, but a suburb holding the overflow of officials and reporters. We were neither. George had come mainly to watch the Games, and I primarily as a tour leader for the *Track & Field News* group of which he was a member. We didn't belong in this village, but despite the armed soldiers posted outside, security was lax.

George and I met outside the gate. A mutual friend, near-Olympian runner and well-established writer Hal Higdon, introduced us. Then together we stormed the gates. Fumbling for credentials we didn't have and pleading ignorance of the guards' Spanish commands, we kept walking toward the inner sanctum. They shrugged and waved us through. Their primary job seemed to keep fellow Mexicans out, not foreigners like us.

Once inside, we joined the stream of residents moving toward the cafeteria. No one challenged us as we took our first breakfast as pseudo-Olympians. George wore Levis, old Tiger Cortez shoes, and a sweatshirt bearing the name of his running club. His face wore the lines of a doctor who'd faced too many midnight crises and a father who'd ridden herd on a dozen children. His hair was thinning and just beginning to gray.

Yet he was one of a new breed—a middle-aged man

who not only ran but raced hard and fast. His reputation as a runner had already started to spread outward from his home base in New Jersey. Here in Olympic Village II, however, he was just an interloper. So was I. Even though I was a junior writer at *Track & Field News*, I fell well short of qualifying for an Olympic press pass.

George and I left the Village together. At the gate, autograph-hunters swarmed to us. I protested in half-remembered high school Spanish that we were nobodies. In broken English, one boy said, "No sir, in Mexico you *muy importante*." We signed, thinking this might be the last time anyone would ever ask.

§ § § § §

George Sheehan was almost fifty years old when we met. His life looked full even before he wrote his first sentence for publication. George would go on to write more and better than anyone in running about all that he thought and felt. The only gaps in his prodigious lifetime output would be reports on all that he'd *done*, especially in all the years before his recorded history. A few early highlights:

• He was the oldest of fourteen children. His father and namesake, George A. Sheehan, was also a physician.

• He shared a coach with Olympic marathon gold-medalist Frank Shorter. Bob Giegengack coached George at a New York City high school and Frank at Yale thirty years later.

• He ran a 4:19 mile for Manhattan College in 1939, when the American record was only thirteen seconds faster. Based on the current mark, his time would now equate to the low-fours.

• He and wife Mary Jane are parents to twelve children. The first, a son and daughter set of twins, were born while George served as a Navy doctor in the Pacific during World War II.

• After completing his Navy tour and residency, he

moved to the Jersey Shore to establish a practice and expand the family.

• George helped found the New Jersey high school that most of his boys attended. The early running of George III and Tim rekindled their dad's interest, dormant for more than twenty years.

A reporter from that area, Robert Cullinane of the *Asbury Park Press*, picks up the story as George would recall it years later:

> He was almost forty-five. A successful cardiologist. A husband and father with a growing brood. A regular in the squash and tennis crowd of Rumson. A man wrapped in the security of a solid, sensible life. But it was the 1960s, and the world was changing. Inside his own world, George Sheehan was changing too.
>
> George recalled, "I was bored, really. Simply bored. I didn't know what I wanted, but I knew I needed a challenge."
>
> He began hanging around the cross-country course and track at Christian Brothers Academy, the school he helped found. Two of his sons, George III and Tim, ran for the school at the time. Dr. George said, "I watched them, and I thought, 'I wonder how I can do compared to them,' I started running almost immediately."
>
> At first he felt shy about being seen running, so he trained in the privacy of his own spacious backyard. But he soon outgrew the ten-laps-to-the-mile course at home. He then graduated to the streets of his tree-lined neighbhorhood in Rumson.
>
> "I would run down Rumson Road in my longjohns. They didn't have any running clothes back then," he said. "My kids were embarrassed. They begged me, " 'Can't you do that where no one will see you?'"
>
> He smiled at the memory. "Imagine," he said.
>
> Imagine indeed. It was the start of his new life. A life as a runner, author, philosopher, record-setter, adviser, and inspiration for the millions who followed in his footsteps.

§ § § § §

But that would all come later. Much later.

George Sheehan started running, as all runners do, for the most personal of reasons. He began with the simple goal of bettering himself. One of his earliest pieces to talk about himself tells what happened to him in 1963. It would stand as one of his classics:

> At the age of reason, I was placed on a train, the shades drawn, my life's course and destination already determined. At the age of forty-five I pulled the emergency cord and ran out into the world. It was a new decision that meant no less than a new life, a new course, a new destination. I was born again in my forty-fifth year.
>
> The previous "me" was not me. It was a self-image I had thrust upon me. It was the person I had accepted myself to be, but I had been playing a role. In time, we can't fool even ourselves. Sooner or later, however, we come to question the trip planned for us, the goals we were given, our itinerary to death. Sooner or later the self-image becomes not worth preserving. The person we are presumed to be seems unsatisfactory and inadequate. Sooner or later, it becomes important that we feel important and have the feeling that what we are doing is important.
>
> When I stepped off that train, I had lost my sense of purpose, my faith in what I was doing, my caring for creation and its creatures. And when I stepped from that train, I found I was not alone.
>
> Millions of Americans who had been told Sunday after Sunday to be born again were now going through the shattering experience of rebirth. Only the experts don't call it that. They call it "middle-aged melancholia" or a "new cultural phenomenon of the fourth and fifth decade," or more simply "change of life."
>
> The authorities agree that we come upon this stage of our life unprepared for the reality of advancing years and receding rewards. White-collar worker, blue-collar worker, housewife and career woman—no one seems immune to the crisis that sets in after the forties get underway. Each of us in our own way comes to this revelation and faces the problem of living according to the person we really are.

Finding one's reality does not come without plan or effort. Being born again is no easy task. Technique and training and much hard work are needed. And we are always faced with the knowledge that it is an undertaking that will never be completed. Every day will be a fresh start.

Most experts suggest we make a new start in a new career, develop new interests. I say begin at the beginning.

Begin with the body. The body mirrors the soul and the mind, and is much more accessible than either. Become proficient at listening to your body, and you will eventually hear from your totality—the complex, unique person you are.

I did it that way. I stepped off that train and began to run. And in that hour a day of perfecting my body, I began to find out who I was. I discovered that my body is a marvelous thing, and learned that any ordinary human can move in ways that have excited painters and sculptors since time began.

I didn't need the scientists to tell me that man is a microcosm of the universe, that he contains the ninety-two elements of the cosmos in his body. In the creative action of running, I became convinced of my own importance, certain that my life had significance.

Fitness may have had something to do with this. The physiologists have shown us that those who remain the perpetual athlete are two and even three decades younger physically than their contemporaries. And with this comes an awareness, a physical intelligence, a sensual connection with everything around you that enlarges your existence.

If decreases in the body's functions are due to non-use and not to aging, is it unreasonable to suggest that our mental and psychological and spiritual capabilities deteriorate the same way? If so, our rebirth will be a long and difficult task. It will begin with the creative use of the body, in the course of which we must explore pain and exhaustion as closely as pleasure and satisfaction. It will end only when we have stretched our mind and soul just as far.

But there is an alternative. You can always get back on that train.

§ § § § §

None of these discoveries came to George Sheehan as quickly as he describes them. He took five years of running and a couple more years of writing to find the words above.

His start in running wasn't quite as lyrical as he describes it. It began partly because of tennis. He broke his racquet hand in a fit of anger after a bad game, and needed a substitute exercise while it healed.

When he resumed running for the first time since college, he was too embarrassed to be seen on the streets. So he laid out a ten-laps-per-mile track around his backyard and ran there until his running outgrew this home course. He then begged his way into races with high school boys. How could the coach turn away a major benefactor of the school?

In 1963, he ran a cross-country race in New York City that was limited to runners over forty. (It has since been called the country's first masters race.) Most runners were quite young then, and most of them wondered, "What are those old guys doing still running?" He dropped out of his first marathon, hitting the wall at seventeen miles in Philadelphia. He then entered his first Boston Marathon in 1964 and finished at about 3:10.

I actually spent a day near George at Boston three years later. He was an oldtimer there by then, and I—at half his age—was a neophyte running my first marathon anywhere. We stood on the same starting line, wearing race numbers 84 and 85, in a crowd that numbered only six hundred. We remember talking to some of the same people that day, but neither of us recalls seeing the other.

Our paths didn't join until Mexico City in October 1968. By then, I was moonlighting as a columnist for a tiny magazine called *Distance Running News*. George's almost-as-small local newspaper had asked him to write a column about his Olympic experience. The magazine would come to be known as *Runner's World*. George's first newspaper column would be but a warm-up act for all that would follow.

E S S A Y

BROTHER GEORGE

BY SISTER MARY SHEEHAN

When we were growing up and asked other kids about their families, they would say something simple like, "There are four of us, two brothers and two sisters."

Then they would ask how many we had in our family. We would start a recital. "George, Arlene, Joan, Jim, Jack, Pat, Mary, Ann, Fran, Skip, Honey, Margie, Liz, Michael. There are sixteen in all, counting our mother and father."

As I was preparing to tell about George as a boy, I called our brothers and sisters and said, "Think of some funny stories about him." After not hearing from them, I phoned again. They told me, "He wasn't funny."

George, the oldest child, was our tour guide. We used to come down to the Jersey Shore from Brooklyn. We called it "going to the country." When we got down to our house at the Shore, George wouldn't allow us to sit down. He would have us playing games from morning to night. Everyone always wanted to be on his team, because he always won. He made the rules.

George lived on the top floor of our house in Brooklyn, a five-story brownstone. He was way, way up. Our mom's job in the morning was to wake him up. They had rigged up a system with a cord reaching all the way to a bell over his bed on the fifth floor. She would pull the cord, not knowing that he had stuffed towels in the bell to muffle it. Then the rest of us who were trying to sleep would waken to her saying, "Let me hear your footfalls, dear." Or else she'd say, "Don't let the darkness deceive you. It's time to get up."

In our family, there was a difference between the way boys and girls were treated. If I came home late from school and was late for dinner, I would go in the kitchen and get my own meal. If George came home late from school, he would go in the dining room and sit down at the dining room table, waiting to be served. I think he tried that when he got married, and Mary Jane immediately let him know that theirs was another kind of family.

Thinking back on our family life, I remember our dining room. We sat in age order, our dad at the end and our mom next to him to protect him. The boys sat on one side of the table and the girls on the other. George was learning Latin and Greek in high school. He would speak Latin and Greek words and phrases to us at the table. We thought this was marvelous, although we didn't understand him. Maybe some of his fans have that experience when they read some of his articles. Even if they don't completely understand him, they think the words and phrases sound marvelous.

Sister Mary Sheehan, a Catholic nun, is one of George's thirteen siblings.

CHAPTER 2
FIRST WRITING

About five years ago, Bob Anderson dreamed up the idea of starting a magazine devoted to his favorite sport. His only qualification was that he liked to run and read about running. Anderson was just a high school senior at the time, one who hadn't yet taken a journalism class. His idea sounded like a teenager's fantasy, and the oldtimers of the sport told him so when he solicited their opinions.

"We already have *Long Distance Log* covering road racing," they said. "And *Track & Field News* covers all the other events. There isn't room for another magazine."

Anderson thanked them for their advice, then ignored it. In 1966, he launched *Distance Running News*.

He nursed the magazine along as a full-time staff of one in its early years. He worked first from his bedroom in Overland Park, Kansas, then his student housing at Kansas State University, then from a small office in Manhattan (the one in Kansas, not New York City). Anderson quit the Kansas State track team, then the school itself, to meet the growing time demands of his magazine. By 1969, he alone served a subscriber list of about two thousand. He needed help in the office.

I worked for *Track & Field News* in California at the time, but also wrote a column for Anderson's magazine. He called me from Kansas to ask, "Would you like to become my editor?"

He offered the chance to specialize in my first love, long-distance running, and to work only with the people I knew best, the road racers. "Of course I'd like the job," I told him. "But I'm settled out here in California and don't want to move back to the Midwest."

"That's fine," said Anderson. "Stay where you are. I've been looking for an excuse to move out there anyway."

He packed his business into a U-Haul and landed in Mountain View as the 1970s began. I started working for him the first week of the new decade.

My first call for new writers went out to George Sheehan. He'd served his apprenticeship in print by now, but this was his first chance to write for an audience made up entirely of runners.

§ § § § §

George Sheehan's hometown newspaper, the *Red Bank Daily Register*, asked him to write about what he saw at the Olympic Games in Mexico City. In what would become trademark Sheehan style, his article ranged far afield from the facts about who won which race in what time. He also introduced the noisy breathing technique which would become another of his trademarks. Here's how his writing career started, with an article published October 19, 1968:

> My father-in-law, who sang in Father Finn's Famous Boys' Choir when he was a youngster in Chicago, once told me that he spent the first three months of instruction without singing a note. He was being taught how to breathe.
>
> It now looks as if breathing doesn't come naturally for runners either. Carl Slough, a specialist in breathing who has been working with U.S. Olympic athletes, contends that they are underusing their involuntary breathing muscles and overusing the voluntary ones.
>
> Expert Slough, who has done dramatic work in treating emphysema patients at the West Haven (Connecticut) Veterans Administration Hospital, believes that runners can be taught to coordinate the respiratory mechanism by instruction and demonstration of what they are doing wrong. By applying light pressure to the chest and abdomen, Slough is able to teach a synchronous response in inhalation. Then the athlete makes a noise or

grunt, starting the descent of the ribs and intake of the abdomen, which accomplishes the exhalation.

Tom Farrell, who made the U.S. Olympic team, and steeplechasers Barry Brown and Pat Traynor, who didn't, believe they have been able to do faster and better work than they ever have done because of Slough's tutoring.

Many runners have been using this Slough technique without knowing it. The expiratory puff of Oregon half-miler Wade Bell is well-known, and anyone who has run with Ted Corbitt, a veteran international distance runner, knows that he emits a grunt or groan for every breath of a marathon's twenty-six-plus miles. An early and rudimentary form of this method in medicine was to have the emphysema patient breathe out against resistance—in this case a soda straw.

Here in Mexico City, the volume and efficiency of intake and output of expired air is secondary to the fact that there is just not enough oxygen in the air itself. But Slough is undoubtedly going to help athletes run faster here and at sea level. Ultimately because of this experiment, his revolutionary concepts will be used for the common good—not only for patients but also for those who seek maximum physical fitness.

The Olympic Games have never become as we once hoped: the moral equivalent of war. What they may become is the *medical* equivalent of war, if the fallout of medical advances of human physiology gained here is any criterion.

Those who say Jim Ryun put Kipchoge Keino away in the U.S.–British Commonwealth meet in Los Angeles last year might find it hard to believe that Keino rates a slight favorite over America's great middle-distance runners in the Olympic 1500-meter race this week. This is partly due to Ryun's bout with mononucleosis, which interfered with his training schedule. But it is mainly because Keino's natural habitat is seven thousand feet high in Kenya, while Ryun hails from the American prairie.

In no other event is the problem of altitude and performance more dramatically posed. Both men already are legends in their time, with Ryun in top form practically unbeatable, and Keino a phenomenal performer through distance ranges wider than any other world-class runner.

Keino has proven what should have been obvious since

the start of experiments on high-altitude adaptation: The best way to adapt is to be born there. Any other method, and especially the short-term efforts of our Olympic squad at Lake Tahoe, should be only an approximation.

A summary of the altitude training of Dr. David Dill confirms this reasoning. Dill reports that performance time for the mile worsened by 3.6 percent the fourth day and 1.5 percent on the twenty-sixth day. The maximum oxygen consumed was lower by 14.6 percent on the second day and 9.5 percent on the twenty-seventh day.

What would that mean in performance after a month's training at high altitude? Well, a four-minute miler would run 4:03.6. At that rate, Herb Elliott's 1500-meter Olympic record of 3:35.6 is safe even with a superb effort by Ryun, whose world record is 3:33.1.

Keino, who no more needs instruction in breathing than a young fish has to be taught to breathe in water, presents a formidable figure to any sea-level athlete. But even he could be surprised.

The 1500-meter Olympic record at Mexico City may be a physical impossibility. But what the world's distance men will do in the record books when they come down from the sky will be awesome to behold.

It remains for some enlightened and far-thinking promoter to transport these men en masse to a sea-level Tartan track at 70-degree temperature and 30-percent or less humidity immediately after the final *adios* rings out and "See you in Munich 1972" flashes across the scoreboard of the Olympic Stadium. That would be a true measure of the men of the XIX Olympiad.

Kipchoge Keino set an Olympic record of 3:34.9 while winning the gold medal at Mexico City. Jim Ryun finished a distant second with a still-creditable time of 3:37.8.

§ § § § §

I knew George Sheehan's writing from the start. He made sure of that.

"The first few were assorted sports pieces—profiles of Gil Hodges, Casey Stengel, the Boston Celtics," Jonathan Black would recall in a profile for *The Runner* magazine. "But as his passion shifted to running, so did his column. Obviously delighted with his new-found pursuit, he photocopied each piece and dispatched it to forty-odd friends."

This became George's self-published newsletter, mailed almost weekly in the late 1960s. I made his mailing list.

His newspaper column evolved a tone of its own. "Being a Catholic-school graduate," he would later tell Robert Cullinane of the *Asbury Park Press*, "I had an aversion to using the word 'I' in my columns. So I created a character I called the Longtime Jogger. I would interview him about things like Earth Day, miniskirts, whatever." Soon, though, George stepped out from behind his alter ego. His writing grew increasingly personal.

"When he got stuck—when his own words didn't adequately express his feelings—he turned to his friends," said Cullinane. "Thoreau, Emerson, William James, Rainer Maria Rilke, Ortega y Gasset."

George worked out early the mix of columns that would serve him well through the years. Some medical advice, some training tips, some racing experiences, and always the Sheehan philosophy. He could dash off a medical or training column—"the nuts and bolts stuff," he called it—in an hour. The "think pieces, the ones I love" might be a whole week taking shape. He said of the deeper pieces, "I need three hours of running for every page of writing. I do my thinking on the run, then I get back home and immediately write these things down before I forget them."

Speaking for the fledgling magazine, now renamed *Runner's World*, I asked George to write not one but two columns. One would give medical advice to readers who presented him with their symptoms. The other column would be an essay. "We can't pay you yet," I told him. "None of the writers is paid at this point." George said that didn't matter. Writing was his hobby, not his business. "You don't have to answer every medical letter," I said. "Just choose those you want to print." He answered every one, paying his own postage.

§ § § § §

George Sheehan's first *Runner's World* columns appeared in the March 1970 issue, my first as editor. He gave the magazine new credibility because he had so much of it himself. He wrote to runners with more authority than other writers because he was a doctor. He wrote with more authority than other doctors because he was a world-record-setting runner, having set a mile mark of 4:47 for fifty-year-olds.

The editor's note under his first *RW* essay read: "George Sheehan is a practicing physician, a cardiologist. But the fifty-one-year-old New Jerseyan's interest and understanding aren't by any means limited to medical topics. A regular newspaper columnist, his writings are rich in literary and philosophical illustrations. His contributions are a welcome addition to our pages."

Here was the Sheehan his readers would come to know and love. Expressing an unusual idea, giving it a surprising plot twist, explaining its meaning, and quoting a master.

This month's idea: "Runners are wondering whether that satisfaction is enough. Their sport has survived charges that it is dangerous (Dr. Harry Johnson of the Life Extension Institute found that twenty-nine of thirty cardiologists in his survey recommended against running for sedentary men over fifty), boring (*The New Yorker* has called it 'a pastime of overpowering ennui'), and intellectual (The American Medical Association says the 'burden of proof still rests with those who state that running will prevent coronary disease').

"Now they are being told running is safe, interesting

and effective—but unnecessary. It can be replaced by something as simple as hypnosis."

George's surprising twist: Canadian physicians tested two groups of post-coronary heart patients, one with a program of daily running and the other in hypnotic trances, imagining themslves running. The results after a year? Identical improvement in both groups. Weight and body fat down, increase in grip strength and EKG tracings, lowering of blood pressure and lessening of the adrenaline production by the body. "Should these findings shake runners down to their arch supports? Of course not. If they keep their cool, they can see what all this means."

So what's the meaning, George? "It means, for one thing, that heart disease and nervous tension are intimately connected. John Hunter, who first described coronary disease and was himself a sufferer, wrote, 'I am at the mercy of any fool who can aggravate me.'

"This notion of stress and irritation was echoed recently by a leading German heart specialist, Berthold Kern. He blames 'agitation and aggravation'—and not obesity, excessive cigarette smoking, and high cholesterol—for heart attacks."

He recruited one of his literary friends, e.e. cummings, to add weight to his own thesis. George quoted a cummings poem:

> little man
> in a hurry
> full of an
> important worry
> halt stop forget delay
> wait

The paradox of running, said George, is that moving rather quickly for an extended distance can serve to slow down one's life. He contended that hard, physical, absorbing work can be as relaxing and refreshing as settling into a trance.

E S S A Y

MANHATTAN MAN

BY GENE MCCABE

I first became aware of George Sheehan in high school. He and I were competitors for schools that were, at the time, almost always going head to head for the Catholic high schools' cross-country championship in New York City. His name, like mine, was a small blip in the fine-print list that might run fifty or one hundred names.

Not until we both arrived at Manhattan College did I begin to notice George emerging from the pack. And emerge he did in many ways—culturally and socially as well as athletically.

Our coach was the legendary Pete Waters, who years before had himself been a leading figure in middle-distance running in the New York area. Pete was a stern taskmaster and a formidable presence. His severe approach and strong discipline worked wonders, and he was able to transform a small school into one of the Eastern powers in track and cross-country. He was also adept at taking the proverbial ninety-seven-pound weakling and turning him into a strongman. That is essentially what he accomplished with George Sheehan.

Manhattan was known in those years for its strength in the middle-distance relays, and there were meets in Madison Square Garden every other week or so during the indoor season. The midweek time trials on the Manhattan oval to determine the makeup of our relay teams frequently produced competition that dwarfed the actual Saturday-night races at the Garden.

What I remember most about George was his barely making the relay team each week, usually with the slowest time of the four runners, then turning in the fastest leg of the team on Saturday night. If such is possible, he would consistently outperform his own physiological capabilities. Though totally spent at the end of the race, he could, if the meet situation called for it, double back forty or fifty minutes later with another top performance.

Coaches love that kind of performer, and Pete Waters was no exception. George was one of the few guys on the team who could bring a twinkle to the coach's eye and even elicit a rare compliment.

George had the misfortune to be in college the same years as a good friend and crosstown rival, Les MacMitchell of New York University. Les was to the college scene approximately what Glenn Cunningham was to the world arena, and over a four-year span George acquired a lot of silver medals that would have been gold if Les had been a few years older or younger.

On a team basis, however, Manhattan won many IC4A and Metropolitan Intercollegiate championships in track and cross-country during George's years there. Away from the track, George was beginning to furnish glints of the qualities that would in later years distinguish his career.

He wrote well and humorously for the *Quadrangle*, the college's weekly newspaper. But perhaps more significantly, especially for an athlete, he contributed often to the *Quarterly*, the college's literary magazine. He wrote learned articles on the Southern poets (Sidney Lanier was one of his favorites) and, of course, on the Irish greats (Yeats, Joyce, O'Casey, Shaw, et al). His writings—and conversations, for that matter—were loaded with that wry, subtle humor that permeated his life.

On the social scene, George was for a long time a shy, bumbling nonstarter when it came to matters like girls and proms and tea dances. But here also he demonstrated that the early going in a long-distance race is not nearly so important as the homestretch. In a typical whirlaway finish, George came from well off the pace and amazed the entire East Coast when he won the hand of the beautiful Mary Jane Fleming.

Gene McCabe, George's Manhattan College teammate, came down the Jersey Shore to share the same hometown of Rumson for many years.

CHAPTER 3

FIRST SPEAKING

George Sheehan is a heart specialist, and his patients think he's a good one. Yet "doctor" is one of the last things I think of when picturing George.

Runner, yes. He's fast enough to be the world's best miler for his age and durable enough to run marathons.

Writer, absolutely. He's good enough to cause *New York Post* columnist Larry Merchant to say, "The best practicing athlete-journalist may be George Sheehan.

Practicing eccentric, to be sure. George, dressed in longjohns and ski mask, once ran past a family moving into his New Jersey neighborhood. They stared at him. He shouted, "Go back! Everyone in this town is crazy!"

I see George lots of ways. But somehow I can't imagine him examining patients. He doesn't fit the white-coat image of a doctor. He shuns the titles, language, appearances, and conventions of his profession. In a field that trains its people in scientific reasoning and laboratory-tested fact, George ventures guesses and trusts what he learns in his "experiment of one." More cautious doctors who read what he writes sometimes criticize him for this. That's okay, he says, because he has criticism for them in return.

George once asked me not to use the letters "MD" on his nonmedical articles. "Some doctors wear the title as if they were born with it," he said. Another time, he mentioned that most veteran runners know more than most doctors about treating athletic injuries. "The doctor is educated in the treatment of disease, not in health. Health is a much more difficult subject. Health is the study of the universe."

George had a conventional medical education. He says

he didn't start learning about true health and fitness until he'd been practicing medicine for twenty-odd years. And he didn't learn it then from medical texts but from becoming a runner. Running has been his experiment-of-one lab. He has learned to treat athletic injuries by treating his own. And running has radically changed his views of human physical potential and aging. More than this, though, it has helped him find the person he always wanted to be and was meant to be.

"Running," he has written, "frees me from the monosyllabic inanities of my usual tongue-tied state, liberates me from the polysyllabic jargon of my profession, removes me from the kind of talk which aims at concealing rather than revealing what is in my heart."

George was meant to write. He has written steadily for more than five years. Now comes his time to branch out as a speaker, opening before a medical audience. Few of the professionals attending the seminar in San Francisco carry the title MD. This program mainly appealed to DPMs, doctors of podiatric medicine. Not all MDs understand or appreciate the iconoclastic George Sheehan. His messages amuse, confuse or enrage many of his colleagues.

But the podiatrists have loved him ever since he started writing that the foot is the root of most running injuries. Podiatrists specialize in problems of the feet. They invited this man they think of as "Saint George" to deliver the keynote speech at a podiatric sports-medicine conference. It was his first major appearance onstage. He appeared in a faded blue shirt with a frayed, button-down collar. A paper clip held his narrow tie in place. George forgot his reading glasses ($2 Woolworth's specials), so he spoke without notes. He started by saying, "I'm not here as a doctor but as an athletes' representative."

He was here to talk about the growing role of feet—and foot doctors—in sports medicine, but he breezed past that subject and into what he really wanted to talk about: the Sheehan Philosophy. The audience, somewhat numbed by a string of clinical lectures, delighted in his light yet deep presentation. He in turn reveled in the applause and decided he'd like to do more speaking if the chance arose.

§ § § § §

Mountain View, home of *Runner's World*, is a San Francisco suburb. During the trip west to give his first big speech, George Sheehan first visited the office of the magazine for which he'd written since 1970. I sat him down for our first interview during that visit.

George already had outgrown the role of mere writer. Among *RW* readers, he'd become a celebrity. They wanted to know more about him than he'd revealed so far in his columns. This is what he said that day:

> *We know you from your writing as a running doctor, but we don't know about the thirty-year period when you didn't run. What was your life like before you started running?*
>
> Fortunately, I don't remember. One of my friends, psychiatrist Paul Kiell, once asked me that. He said, "George, what was it like before we began running?" I said, "Paul, I'm really not interested."
>
> I don't remember too clearly. But I'm sure it was a void.
>
> I think up until the time I started to run, I was involved in the entire—what shall I say?—conventional, standard approach to life. I realized that it was incomplete, but I thought it was that way because I hadn't reached certain goals. I was forty-four, was living in Rumson, which is one of the richest suburbs of the New York metropolitan area. I had arrived at a certain degree of professional success and economic success. I had a large family, which was doing well.
>
> Yet I seemed to be running in place, so to speak. There were the usual party weekends, blackouts, falling asleep in front of the TV on nights I wasn't on duty. I was stagnating.
>
> *At this point, you're a runner, a doctor, a writer. How do these many different activities mesh for you? Do they supplement each other or conflict?*
>
> I see no conflict. The running, as James Dickey said about poetry, is the hub of my creative wheel. Everything comes out of my running—my writing which is thought out on the run, where I am as an individual,

what I am doing professionally, my relationship to myself, other people, the universe, whatever.

Now I've cut my running down, unfortunately, because I find that at age fifty-five I'm afraid of overdoing. I'm down to three to four runs a week. But the running is the center of my whole living. What I do is planned around that, and it feeds all my other activities.

Most of our readers know you through your writing. How did you develop as a writer?

After I wrote an article for one of my local papers about the Mexico City Olympics, I started to put out a weekly column. In the beginning, I was very cautious about exposing myself and how I felt, or I didn't feel the things I now feel. I think it was a combination. Then I gradually began to find myself—and in the process found philosophers who were saying exactly what I felt but in so much better words.

I view myself as something like a .230 hitter in writing who just happens to be filling a niche. There's no one else around to do it now, but I will be displaced eventually by some Hall of Famer who has a lot more talent. I think I'm hanging in there only by pushing what I have to the absolute limit.

You run three or four days a week, race nearly every weekend, write a weekly column, work as a full-time physician, answer all the calls and letters coming in from runners, keep up a busy family life. How do you find the time?

I have no difficulty finding the day sufficient for that. I have very few other interests. My wife and I have virtually no social life, because I found after I began running that I didn't want to go to parties.

My relationship with other people is now my outstanding problem. A runner comes to be extremely self-sufficient. His world is inside himself. Ideas are much more interesting than people. He becomes an elitist in that sense. Although he recognizes that other people have their truth, he's not the least bit interested.

Why don't you run through your routine for a week?

Monday I devote almost entirely to my practice and usually don't run. Tuesday I run long. It takes me about an hour. During that run, I think out my [newspaper] column.

Wednesday is my day off, and I go to the newspaper office. It takes me about six hours to put that six hundred to eight hundred words into shape. Sometimes if I'm not too clear [on what to write], I have to go out and run for forty-five minutes to an hour before I sit down at the typewriter.

Thursday I run long again. I spend the day at the hospital doing stress tests and reading EKGs, then break at midday for the run.

Friday I go short—maybe a half-hour. I spend that afternoon, along with Monday, in my office. I get six to eight phone calls each of these days from runners all over the country. The week before the Boston Marathon last year, I got a call from a fellow in New Orleans who said, "I think I'm prepared, but should I go out and run another marathon just to make sure?"

Saturday I take off, usually in preparation for a race on Sunday.

Do you ever have trouble walking a thin line between giving general medical advice and giving a specific diagnosis to runners who write and call you?

No, I don't try to walk a thin line. I try to tell them as best I can what I think the diagnosis is, even if it disagrees with the working diagnosis [of their own doctors]. I know the limitations of distance and not being able to talk with the person directly. But having experienced most, if not all, of the problems, I write of that experience plus my medical knowledge. What I found in running is that the vast majority of doctors have no idea how to go about treating an athlete.

You once said you've learned more about sports medicine from being an athlete than from being a doctor.

The only way I learned was to experience these ailments, and then to confirm what other runners have told me. It has been a collaboration between me and the people who've written in to *Runner's World*. Because of this, I think we've made some real breakthroughs. There's really no need now for a runner to go through any prolonged period on the injury list. It's simply a matter of getting the correct information to him.

I had one thing in my favor. I was in the profession and realized that the profession knew nothing. In my years of running, I've never been helped by a doctor with an "MD" behind his name. I ended up with the DPMs [podiatrists] and RPTs [physical therapists], or a person like Paul Uram who is a gymnastics coach.

You've been writing for Runner's World for several years now. What do you consider the most important sports-medicine advances in that time?

The most significant is the recognition that the biomechanically weak foot is the major cause of all foot and leg injuries in runners. Since 30 percent of the people have weak feet—what I call "Morton's foot"—and 80 to 90 percent of the people who get in trouble have it, it is a major problem in runners.

The second major finding is that training actually puts the runner at hazard. When you train, three things happen and two of them are bad. The two things that are bad are that the flexibility of the prime-movers [major working muscle] is being impaired, and a relative weakness develops in the antagonistic muscles. Athletes are at more hazard than nonathletes for muscle and tendon injuries.

So what I'm saying is that the major difficulties are this structural weakness in the foot, which we are born with, and this postural weakness or imbalance, which we develop through training. The two in combination cause 95 percent of our problems. The only way these things can be corrected is to get to the root through proper control of the foot and proper exercise.

Some doctors have criticized you for being "simplistic" or have said that your conclusions are "unfounded personal opinion." How do you respond to this?

Just because a thing is simple doesn't mean it isn't right. The basic principles by which things operate are usually quite simple. There's no question that the foot is an extremely complicated organ. I think the principle that a weakness here causes the difficulty is not a simplistic thing to say.

It's very complicated for the podiatrists to pick out what this weakness is and what to do about it. But the simplicity of the formula—structural instability plus postural instability equals overuse syndrome—proves that it's correct.

Let's talk a bit about the Sheehan Philosophy—your non-

medical ideas about running. There are some apparent contradictions. First you have said running has changed your life for the better, yet you say running is not for everyone. Can you explain?

There are only a few people who are true runners. Others might be frustrated in it. So I don't try to sell running.

One of our main problems in leisure is finding the correct sport, finding the sport that is tuned into our constitution and personality and temperament. The true runner is a very fortunate person. He has found something that is just perfect for him.

How would you describe a "true runner"?

These are people to whom ideas are very important, who don't socialize well, who for the most part have the correct build. I believe nature constructs you for certain activities, and the activity you're best constructed for is the one you should probably do.

Psychologically, since I react to stress by withdrawing, since I go to my room when I get bad news, I find that running alone on the roads is something I enjoy very much. I feel that I'm in my right environment.

The second apparent contradiction: Although you are a physician, you tend to play down the health benefits of running and stress instead of the psychological.

Perhaps I do, but I think there are great health benefits from running. I always try to stress that I am a totality and that physical fitness is only part of the entire picture. As fitness improves, so do the mind and spirit. From fitness flows the other benefits.

A third conflict: You obviously enjoy running, and yet an underlying theme in your writing is the suffering involved.

I'm sure that you have to challenge yourself from time to time. You have to find your limits. If you don't do that, if you just go out and enjoy yourself, you forget the struggle you're in. Life is a struggle, and we need to do those things to ourselves to find out what we can stand.

Running provides happiness, which is different from pleasure. Happiness has to do with struggling and enduring and accomplishing. Running provides that sense of being alive, of handling things, of having gone through the initiation.

E S S A Y

ORIGINAL SPLENDOR
BY MARY JANE SHEEHAN

Fifty years ago, I fell in love with a slightly built man in a seersucker jacket. After we were married and we had six months together, he was sent to the South Pacific as a Navy doctor. That's probably the last six months we ever had one on one.

He returned home eighteen months later to a wife and two children, and he was gone most of the time doing his medical residency. When we came to Red Bank, he had four children and was gone from seven o'clock in the morning until nine o'clock at night, taking care of everyone else's household.

Within a couple of years, as his practice grew, I discovered that he not only had paid off the mortgage but there was $10,000 in the bank. And we had been living on $450 a month with five children. I decided that from then on this would be a different story. Long before Hillary Clinton gave it credibility, we had a liberated marriage. We gave each other the freedom to do what we both liked to do best.

I have been waiting twenty years to answer some of the great quotations that runners have lived with and thrived on. The first one is, "I have no upper-body strength." And he didn't.

On the day when the garbage was to be carried out, he was so thrown off-balance that it would either fall on the floor or splat on the staircase. After a half-hour of yard duty, he would come in blistered and bleeding. Yet he was running three- and four-hour marathons.

If you asked him to take the children, he would make a beeline for his mother's house. He knew that she and his sisters would take care of the children while he watched a ballgame. Later, when his grandchildren visited, he made a beeline upstairs and hid under the bed.

However, when he was working, he gave his all—which

in turn gave him an ulcer. That ulcer then started to wear on George, and it wasn't long before he started to become angry with his patients. He didn't like taking responsibility for their lives.

He was coming home to teenagers on the phone, little boys playing hockey in the kitchen, four kids in college with eight to go. No, he didn't "get off the train," as he has written about his beginning to run. He got off of 25 Rumson Road.

From then on, he "took life into his own hands, made new rules, went back to his body, became a good animal." He would crawl up the stairs, grunting and groaning with exhaustion.

Every Saturday, every Sunday, he was off running races. He was never home.

He became interested in the group of masters he was running with. Before long, attractive young women were running alongside the masters. And it wasn't long before these men were "taking their lives into their own hands and making new rules." This was "man fully functioning, out there taking risks."

However, when the disease struck, the child in George came out. He realized that the old rules were quite comforting and pleasant to be with, and he returned to home and family. My favorite quote comes from one of George's books: "It's not our original sin that we should be concerned about, but our original splendor as God created and called us to."

This is what George always did. Although he was well endowed with great genes from a bright mother and a compassionate father, George went further and never once gave in to his needs instead of the needs to find truth and better ways to do things—whether it was in his own scholarship, whether it was for his patients, or whether it was for his children. For this, his children and I honor and thank him.

Mary Jane Fleming married George Sheehan in 1944, and together they had twelve children.

FIRST BOOK

Charlie Attwood, a pediatrician and marathoner, decided three years ago to move his family from California back to his native South. While scouting for small- to medium-sized towns, Dr. Attwood reached Crowley.

He naturally wanted to take a run here to check out its suitability as a home course. Almost as soon as he set foot on these tree-shaded streets, the local police stopped him. "Two of them put me in their car and questioned me," he recalls. "They weren't belligerent. They'd just never seen a grown man running before, and they wondered what I was doing."

He moved here anyway and, within a year, Attwood had most of the police force supporting running in Crowley by directing traffic at the races he directed.

Before his arrival, there had been no races of note between Houston and New Orleans (Crowley is about equal distance from each), so the doctor started one. He tied it in with a local celebration and called it the International Rice Festival Marathon. In only its third running, this event hosted the national championship. "If this can happen here in Crowley," says Attwood, "it can happen anywhere. This was about the most nonrunning area you could find, and yet we've been able to get the whole town turned on to this race."

Coming into town, you notice a highway sign announcing: "Crowley: Cleanest City in Louisiana! Population 17,121." This is the heart of Cajun country. Creole French is the first language in many homes. Business signs and mailboxes show many family names ending in "x." Restaurants feature crawfish and rice dishes. Rice is the money crop here. It grows in the wet, lush flatlands between Crowley (where the race finishes) and Lafayette (its starting point), and October is harvest time. The locals celebrate with an event of some importance in the area, the Rice Festival. The marathon is a newcomer to the celebration which includes concerts, a carnival, and parade. In three years, the race has advanced from being one of the freaky sideshows to the main event for bringing in outsiders.

"There have been a few complaints from the farmers that we're trying to turn their event into what they call 'a big track meet,'" says Attwood. "But in general we've been able to convince them that the race is good for the overall festival and the town."

Crowley is the second-smallest town ever to host a national marathon. And this is the race's first visit to the South. The town combines the traditional Old South with the progressive New South, the subject of a recent full issue in *Time* magazine. The Attwood home symbolizes this combination. It's a plantation-style mansion built at the turn of the century. Frances Parkinson Keyes used it as a setting for her novel, *Blue Camellia*. But in back of the proud old house sits a new swimming pool, along with a hot tub. This home housed many of the race guests, chief among them George Sheehan. Dr. Attwood pulled another coup by luring George away from bigger-city events to down here. By now, he is the most sought-after speaker on the running circuit.

George is one of the reasons why running has spread to places like this one. His voice, both spoken and in his writings, now carries to all corners of the country.

§ § § § §

Frank Shorter, the Olympic gold- and silver-medalist in the marathon, paid George Sheehan something of a compliment when he complained about his conversations with some runners. Shorter said, "I don't want to talk about Dr. Sheehan all the time."

George has become one of the most-talked-about figures in the sport. In name recognition, he now ranks alongside the medal-winners and record-setters. And why not? He's more visible and accessible than most bigtime athletes.

The readers and listeners see George as one of them. True, he's fast for his age but never one of the overall winners. He's one of this generation's runners, whose pace and age set them apart from the young winners. Most of today's runners have a hard time identifying with Frank Shorter, so far removed are his efforts from their own. But they see themselves clearly in the words of George Sheehan, such as:

"For every runner who tours the world running marathons, there are thousands who run to hear the leaves and listen to the rain and look to the day when it all is suddenly as easy as a bird in flight. For them, sport is not a test but a therapy, not a trial but a reward, not a question but an answer."

These lines appeared early in George's recent book, *Dr. Sheehan on Running*. He calls it his first book, but this takes some explaining.

Runner's World published a Booklet of the Month series to supplement the magazine through the first half of the 1970s. The June 1972 booklet carried George's byline. It was grandiosely titled (by me, not George) the *Encyclopedia of Athletic Medicine*. George wrote some of the advice and approved the contributions from other writers, but he never claimed full parenthood for this work.

The monthly *Runner's World* booklets gave way to the *Runner's Book Series* in 1975. *RW* chose its number-one writer, George Sheehan, to write the first book. He would always refer to it as "my first" as well. *Dr. Sheehan on Running* pulled together about one hundred of his newspaper and magazine columns. "I can't sit down and write a book," George had said. "All I can do is keep writing my six hundred to eight hundred–word pieces and hope they will grow into a book." This book quickly became running's bestseller to date. It placed George in even greater demand than before as a writer and speaker, and made him ask more of himself.

He told me repeatedly, "The reaction to this book is so good that it's scary. I've said about all I have to say, and publishers are asking me for another book. How can I top this one?"

§ § § § §

George Sheehan spoke on Friday, the day before the marathon, in Crowley. He was the center of attention at a party that night at the Attwood home. "I've had a cold for nearly a month," he said at the party. "I'm not running tomorrow." Then he took another sip of beer before adding, "But I always think that the night before a marathon. I may just wake up in the morning, see it's a good day, and decide to run."

Saturday morning, George stood in the predawn rain at Lafayette, ready to run, the number "1" pinned to his chest. He finished the marathon in good time, won an age-group award, spoke again at the post-race dinner, received another award, enjoyed another party, then limped aboard a plane on Sunday morning for his flight home.

Running a satisfying marathon had the same effect on him as writing an acclaimed book. A brief sunny period of elation, followed by clouds of doubt.

Soon after his run, George again asked himself, "What can I do to top this?" His search for an answer led to his column the next week, an essay seldom if ever topped in the past:

> The flight home was depressing. The weekend in Crowley, Lousiana, had been a peak experience—had been, in fact, the climax of my life as a runner and as a writer, and perhaps as a person. I had worn number "1" in the National Championship Marathon race and finished in the top third of the field.
>
> Before the race, runner after runner had come up and shook my hand, saying, "Dr. SHEE-han, I loved your book and just want you to know it." One said he had

given eighteen copies as Christmas presents. All week-end, runners sought me out to tell me how much I had helped them. Later at the awards dinner, I was given a plaque. I was, the inscription said, the "outstanding distance runner of the year." A similar plaque the previous year had said the same thing about Olympic champion Frank Shorter. I was being classed with the immortals and then, as a final gesture of esteem, I was permitted to talk.

The talk was more than a talk. It was a love affair. I spoke to each face in turn, and saw in each a reflection of my feeling for that person. I told the runners of the beauties of our bodies and how we need play. I told them we were all meant to be heroes in some way, and if we were heroic enough we would see God.

When I finished speaking, I was in tears and so were they. Then we all stood and applauded who we were and what we had done and the feeling that was in that great room.

And now I was flying away from all that. Flying toward what?

Where was I to go from here? What was there to reach for that would surpass where I had been? Where would I get the size and strength and presence to be more than I was that day?

Life, I saw again, was a problem that will never be solved. At no time is this more evident than when we are close to the solution—at no time more evident than when we succeed, when we have come far but not far enough. The wise men have spoken of this. For every hundred of us who can handle adversity, they've concluded, there is but one who can handle success. Flying home, I knew I was not that one.

My elation had disappeared. I was fearful of the future. I had exhausted my potential and could see nothing ahead but repeating what I had already done, doing the few things I did well over and over again for the rest of my life. The man seated next to me on the plane was a runner who had completed his first marathon in Crowley. "What do I do now?" he asked, echoing the thought in my mind. His answer would be my answer.

What do I do now? More of the same—only better. Run another marathon and learn that much more about myself and the world. Run another and another. Bathe myself in pain and fatigue, reach for energies I have yet to use. Run another and another and another. Make my truth out of that experience. What do I do now? No matter what I have done, there is still more to do. No matter how well it has been done, it can still be done better.

I thought then of the ancient Egyptians who believed there was a judgment after death, and the initial step was to weigh the heart. It seems so true. The heart is the measure of our energy, our courage, our intuition, our love. It is the measure of our days, of what we have done, of who we are.

Was I ready, then, to have my heart weighed? Was this as far as I would go? Was I ready to rest, to obey the commandments and await my reward?

The plane was bringing me back to earth. Without thinking, I took my pulse—a slow, steady forty-eight, and only a day after a marathon. I knew then, as every runner knows, that my heart is capable of anything. All it asks is the time to do it.

When I have run my best marathon and written my best piece and done my best deed of love, I know the cry will still come from my heart: "There is more, there is more! I who have made you know."

What else is heart, then, but to be uneasy, to ask for what seems impossible and never be satisfied? My heart will be restless until it finds its final rest. Then they can weigh it.

ESSAY

BODY TALK
BY GEORGE SHEEHAN III

Dad wanted all his sons to go to an all-boys' school as he had. So taking matters into his own hands, doing it his way, he organized the local lay Catholic community to create Christian Brothers Academy in Lincroft, New Jersey. The hidden blessing for the running community was that the Christian Brothers brought along Brother Basilian. He was the George Allen, the Vince Lombardi of cross-country.

Brother Basilian had a tradition of running a cross-country race for all members of the freshman class. Ectomorphs, endomorphs, and mesomorphs all toed the line, and he made sure with a stick that they all got home in a reasonable time.

The two oldest Sheehan boys, Tim and I, were discovered as runners this way. We had always dreamed of being basketball stars so we could play indoors in front of the cheerleaders. Despite all of our long hours of practice, we flat out could not shoot the rock.

Dad had not yet become a runner at this point, but he did follow us religiously. He was there at many of the meets, and his own running consisted of dashing to different points on the course, screaming one word at us: "Relax!"

I have to say that he had a temper in those days. It evaporated over time, once he got into his daily runs. But who wouldn't have a temper with twelve children and in an era when he had to make house calls in the middle of the night? When he got mad, he had a three-word litany: "Shit, piss, and corruption!" If you heard that, you would head for the farthest bedroom in the house. He may have been small, but he had a pretty good right. He also had a rule that he only hit below the belt and from behind.

Dad's big break in running came because of his temper. He broke his hand in a pique of anger after a lousy tennis game. Here he was with a broken hand. What was he going to do if he couldn't play tennis? He decided after chasing Tim and me at our races, "I'm going to try this."

This was 1963 when people who ran in public were accused of running in their underwear. So Dad decided to run in the privacy of his own backyard. He mapped out a mile course, ten loops. I was there on a hot summer day when he ran his first mile. The three-word curse litany dropped the last two words. Anyone who heard him repeat that one word might have thought he suffered from Tourette's syndrome.

Terry Broderick, a classmate of mine at CBA, went on to become the track coach there. He was coaching at the school when Dad was on the verge of breaking the world mile record for fifty-year-olds. "I worked with the distance runners, traditionally the intellectual if not lunatic fringe," Terry tells me. "They worked hard. In addition to the distance work, they did repeat 300-yard sprints on a covered oval in an old horse barn."

Here was Dad, doing these killer workouts of a dozen hard sprints with a ninety-second break after each one. "Even those bright, shining fourteen- to seventeen-year-old faces and bodies would show the considerable strain of these workouts," Terry recalls. "Doc starts showing up for our practices—and races, I might add. The one indelible memory I have of him is those killer workouts.

"He wouldn't make the ninety-second recovery lap after the fifth or sixth 300. While flat on his back or kneeling head down, gasping for air, he would repeat that Zen-like one-word phrase over and over again at this Catholic school. Then with the next hard 300 about to start, he would somehow get to his feet and run right with those kids thirty-five years his junior."

Dad has often been accused of being a plagiarist, but one of his original lines that has lasted is "Listen to your body." The body is truly a marvelous instrument on its own, has its own knowledge and will give you its own signals.

But the trouble is that for thirty years runners had to listen to *him* at races. This sudden attack of profanity after the race was preceded by an horrific series of groans down the finishing straightaway. Many runners have told me, "I heard your father, but I couldn't beat him." These are young guys too.

Dad might not have always listened to his body. But he never failed to listen to his heart.

George A. Sheehan III is Dr. George's eldest son and business manager. He was also an outstanding distance runner at his dad's alma mater, Manhattan College, in the 1960s.

CHAPTER 5

ENJOYING FAME

This time, the scene happened to be Kansas City. But it could just as well have been Boston, Salt Lake City, Omaha, Phoenix, Mountain View, or any number of other cities where George Sheehan and I have visited this wild and wonderful year.

Running is booming. And our careers along with it.

The number of runners has exploded into the millions, and with it the demand for more and better running events. They're growing in number, size, and quality. Sponsors are taking note of this sport's appealing demographics and dropping big money into the races. They now can pay some of their guests to appear. George and I are called on to come and speak to runners almost every weekend, and often in midweek as well. Our books are flying out the doors of stores.

The circulation of *Runner's World* magazine has boomed into the hundreds of thousands. Until recently, *RW* held a national monopoly. Now *The Runner* and *Running Times* compete for the same readership. The general media is even taking an interest in this sport for the first time. Running isn't merely an offbeat sport anymore. It's a full-blown phenomenon.

Our hosts in Kansas City arranged an all-day tour of radio stations, TV studios, and newspaper offices. I followed George from one interview to the next, never getting to say much. George charmed these interviewers, just as he does his running audiences. After talking with him, they might remember, "Oh yes, we also have with us... What's your name again?" I didn't mind. By now, I was used to feeling invisible in George's presence. I enjoyed standing in the wings, watching him perform.

The worst duty a speaker can perform is to come onstage after George. He isn't just a hard act to follow; he makes it impossible. Other speakers now insist that he appear last on a program. I know how they feel, after following him once this year. He packed the auditorium for his talk. When he finished speaking, most of the crowd followed him out the door. Only a few people remained to hear me speak. I told them, "I feel like the janitor, coming here to clean up after the big game has ended."

§ § § §

Kurt Vonnegut, the novelist, once talked about the economics of being a writer. "They get either $50 for something or $500,000," said Vonnegut, "and there doesn't seem to be much in between."

For every half-million-dollar writer, thousands make half a hundred. For every one who makes $50 an article, thousands would pay to have anything in print. It's a funny business. I used to think that all running writers were and always would be $50 people. I was happy to write about my hobby and get paid a little bit for it too. The $500,000 writers were names on bestseller lists. They seemed very remote from me, like comparing the running I did with that of Olympic marathoners. The same basic activity, yes, but far apart in what we made of it.

Then something happened. Running boomed, and suddenly the bestselling authors weren't Olympian anymore. They were my friends.

Jim Fixx went right to the top of the nonfiction list for hardbacks with his *Complete Book of Running*. George Sheehan put his *Running & Being* in the top eight at the same time. Imagine that! Two running books outselling almost everything else on every subject, all because this sport of ours had somehow caught the public's fancy.

The running boom. I don't know when it first took

that name, who named it, exactly when it started, or who was most responsible for launching it. Some say it started in the 1960s with the writings coach Arthur Lydiard (author of *Run to the Top*) and Dr. Kenneth Cooper (*Aerobics*). Some say it began between 1972 and 1976 with the running successes of Frank Shorter (winner of the Munich Olympic marathon) and Bill Rodgers (winner of the Boston and New York City marathons).

This much we do know: The running *book* boom peaked in 1978. Not only did Fixx and Sheehan both occupy the all-topics bestseller list at the same time, but several other running authors also competed for that honor.

"The fish are hungry now," said George, speaking of running readers. "You can throw almost anything into the water now, and they'll bite."

Fixx has sold the most copies with *The Complete Book of Running*. But even he bows to George as being the writer-king of their sport. "If a runner were to find himself on a desert island where he was allowed only one companion, who would it be?" asks Fixx in his chapter on George. "By all odds, the likeliest candidate would be a cardiologist from rural Red Bank, New Jersey, named George A. Sheehan. In the whole world of running, there is no one quite like Sheehan—and certainly no one whose knowledge of running and influence on it is as great."

George also wrote about Jim Fixx and the success of his book:

> Back before running became a phenomenon and he was still at work on his *Complete Book of Running*, he came to interview me. We talked about running and my writing, and he brought up the success of my book, *Dr. Sheehan on Running*. Why, he asked me, had the book sold so well?
>
> It was his idea that my book had something of the quality of that perennial bestseller, Izaak Walton's *The Compleat Angler*. People who have absolutely no interest in fishing continue to read this discourse on "the contemplative man's recreation." They are simply caught up by the author's enthusiasm and encyclopedic knowledge about what many would consider a trivial subject. In retrospect, it is clear that Fixx's book is the present

counterpart of *The Compleat Angler*. His book is a compendium of all the information you would ever need to become a runner.

Fixx is a fine journalist and has in addition a personal involvement, a bias, a zest that journalists are not supposed to have—or at least not show. He is an enthusiast, a true believer, a worthy successor to Walton. His book will stand.

George then shifted to his own books. The latest was his bestselling *Running & Being*:

The enthusiasm is there, God knows. I am also a true believer. But all the research, all the information is concerned with one individual: myself. My book is not journalism; it is a journal. It is about the *feel* of being a runner, the feel of growth, the feel of control, the feel of being at home in what I am doing.

And later George wrote:

A book can never be so badly written, said Mark Twain, that someone won't still claim it saved his life. The letters I receive suggest that my book, despite the quality of its writing, has indeed had an impact on some people's lives. If nothing else, it has offered a validation of their own experiences. My pilgrim's progress has been matched by the progress of every pilgrim among my readers.

When someone asks me to sign one of my books, I find it dogearred and underlined; when a runner tells me that reading my book is like looking in a mirror; when someone says that whole paragraphs of my book had been written in his mind before he saw my words in print, then I know happiness. I have a feeling that I must write another book to express it.

George already was at work on the next book. He would called it *This Running Life*. Jim Fixx was writing the *Second Book of Running*. Dozens of Sheehan and Fixx wannabes were producing books of their own that would soon glut the marketplace.

§ § § § §

Action, reaction. Writers like George Sheehan got their chance to sing the praises of running to a mass audience. Then, inevitably, critics everywhere from the *New York Daily News* and *Washington Post*, to the *Christian Science Monitor* and *Sports Illustrated* took their return shots. The common thread in their essays was a sarcastic, hostile, defensive tone.

The writers all seemed to say, "I don't choose to run. So don't make me feel guilty or try to cram it down my throat."

I expected this in the big newspapers, in reaction to the blizzard of praise. But I hadn't counted on a biting editorial in *Sports Illustrated* by Frank Deford, since he has written many sensitive articles about running. "I am sick of joggers, and I am sick of runners," Deford wrote. "I don't care if all the people in the U.S. are running or planning to run or wishing they could run. All I ask is, don't write articles about running and don't ask me to read them.

"I don't ever again want to read about the joy of running, the beauty, the ecstasy, the pain, the anguish, the agony, the rapture, the enchantment, the thrill, the majesty, the love, the coming-togetherness, the where-it's-atness. I don't ever again want to hear running compared to religion, sex, or ultimate truth."

George Sheehan might be guilty of overstatement, but he hasn't committed the crimes of taking himself too seriously or claiming that he has found ultimate truths.

He laughed louder than anyone when he saw himself parodied in *The New Yorker* magazine. He considered this the ultimate success. *New Yorker* writer Daniel Menaker published an essay titled "Z-ing & Being: A Horizontal Alternative to the Bestseller by Dr. George Sheehan." It satirized the prologue of the book *Running & Being*.

George's original: "There are times when I am not sure whether I am a runner who writes or a writer who runs. Mostly it appears that the two are inseparable. I cannot write without running, and I am not sure I would run if I could not write. They are two different expressions of my person. As difficult to divide as my body and mind."

Menaker's parody: "There are times when I am not sure whether I am a sleeper who spends some of his time awake or someone who is often awake but spends much of his time asleep. I like to think of my sleeping and waking selves as two parts of an inseparable unit, like bunk beds: What is the lower half without the upper, and, especially, what is the upper half without the lower?"

Menaker used a Sheehanesque personal confession about how he had changed his life: "I have made a vocation of slumber because I am not much good at anything else. When I was younger, I was a somnolent outsider... I was always trying to explain myself, to make excuses for myself.

"Those who listened to me always ended up saying, 'Why not give it a rest?' But I fooled them. I took them seriously. I became an endurance sleeper."

The New Yorker humorist used the Sheehan-like short, punchy sentence fragments: "I sleep. Without excuses. Without apology. A lot. As much as I can. And then some more." He quoted literary figures, from Tennyson to Coleridge. Menaker ended, as Sheehan might, with a line from Falstaff: "He was not only sleepy in himself but the cause of sleep in others."

George Sheehan wrote in *Running & Being* about why he runs. He concluded that it isn't for exercise, to find fame or to escape. He essentially runs for the sake of running.

Menaker's version: "Know this—I do not sleep to rest. I do not sleep to awaken. I do not sleep to be famous. I do not sleep to avoid the dentist. I sleep to sleep."

The article absolutely nailed the Sheehan style but all in good fun. George took it in that spirit, sharing copies with friends who didn't otherwise read *The New Yorker*. But he also wouldn't let this fun-poking piece alter the style and content of his writing in the slightest.

E S S A Y

CHILDHOOD MEMORIES
BY PETER, NORA, JOHN, MICHAEL,
AND ANN SHEEHAN

George's longtime friend and fellow New Jersey MD Paul Kiell collected reminiscences from the Sheehan children for the American Medical Athletic Association Quarterly. *"In his last few years," Dr. Kiell writes, "I heard George Sheehan ruminate over what would be his monument, what he could leave of lasting value. He had always played down his role as a parent, but his children had something else to say about that." Here, five of them share memories of their dad when they all were much younger.*

PETER: As a young boy, I asked about his experiences in World War II. Hearing that he had been in a battle, I asked, "What did you do there?" Anticipating something heroic, I heard him reply, "I hid under a mattress."

NORA: I remember a day at the Reds, my father's family beach compound. I was swimming in the ocean and had gone out too far. The waves were pulling me out, crashing on me, and I was terrified. Then I heard a voice calling to me. "I am coming, Nora," Dad screamed, and I saw him tiny in the distance, swimming out to save me, and I wasn't afraid.

He always believed that I would do something special, and his message was, "Do what you love most. The Sheehans are late bloomers." He was always cheering me on, protecting me.

JOHN: I think I'm most thankful to my father for the things he *didn't* do. He was never demanding of me, he never discouraged me, he never doubted me, and he didn't teach me how to tip.

MICHAEL: I was running a cross-country race as a freshman at Red Bank Catholic. A short uphill distance to the finish line and having conceded first place to another runner, I was locked in a battle for second. Giving my all, I still could not break away.

Then as we turned the corner for home, Dad appeared out of nowhere, shouting, "Now, Michael! Take him on the hill!" And I did.

The emotion of that day is still indescribable. As I told him years later, that was the day he became my father and I became his son. It had nothing to do with running—just the pure experience of knowing that around each corner, each threshold in life, he would be there.

ANN: When I was a young girl he took me to track meets. I found the relay the most exciting race. I knew the critical moment was the passing of the baton. In his life, he ran hard and well. Then he passed the baton to us gently and courageously so we wouldn't miss a step.

CHAPTER 6

ENDURING FAME

The morning after. There's always a morning after, when he awakens to find he's not a celebrity but a sixty-two-year-old man badly in need of his first dose of caffeine.

This was a new day, a new week in the first month of a new year, and George Sheehan had to go out and prove himself all over again. He says he welcomes that challenge, but his face said otherwise. George looked tired from a hard weekend in Seattle. He had spoken at a sports-medicine conference on Saturday, raced ten kilometers on Sunday, then talked again after the race.

"I'm in a fog," he said as we met at the Eugene airport. "They gave me a standing ovation after that last talk. Those don't come very often, at least not for me. But I can't remember what I said to deserve it."

Like a runner who just had a great race, George's feelings were mixed. He was proud of the performance but wondered, "What must I do now to top this?" Elation blended with depression right after the cheering stopped.

The man with one of the best-known names and faces in running walked unnoticed through a crowded airport in the city that prides itself on being the nation's running capital. Mary Jane was with him on this trip, and she asked what she could do and see in Eugene this day. George wanted nothing more than a day of rest, but he had flown here instead of home for the sole purpose of being interviewed.

The running boom has spawned a fourth major magazine—called *Running*, sponsored by the Nike shoe company and based here in Eugene. George doesn't work for this magazine, or any longer for *Runner's World*. Several *RW* writers defected last year in a dispute over book royalties. George went to *The Runner*, while I chose *Running* magazine. I brought up the idea of interviewing him with my editor, figuring Paul Perry would nix it for promoting a competitor. But Perry said, "A few people are bigger than who they work for, and George Sheehan is one of them."

Runners are attracted to George the way news viewers think of Walter Cronkite—not because his information is that much different from other commentators' but because of how it is delivered. Sheehan, like Cronkite, calms and reassures his audiences. They feel as comfortable with him as they would with a kindly and wise old uncle.

But poke through George's public manner and you find a man who works very hard at making it all look easy. He speaks nearly a hundred times a year but still gets so nervous before going onstage that he can hardly remember his own name. He writes a column each week for his local newspaper, revising it as many as four times—"then once more for spontaneity."

This pace left him tired this Monday morning, but he told me, "I'm yours for the day."

George popped the top of a diet cola and sat down before the tape recorder. The fatigue began slipping from his face as soon as the tape rolled.

§ § § § §

Why do you travel so much and speak so often when it seems to be such hard work?

I'm trying to get my thoughts in the air or on paper so people will be influenced by them. I once had this feeling: Why go across the country and spend two or three days, and eventually speak to five hundred or one thousand people total? In that same period of time, I might write something that a million people would read. It seemed silly to do those trips.

But then I found that if I didn't go out and speak, I didn't have anything to write about. I would say about a third of my columns have their origin in something that occurred on a trip or in a race. I cannot just sit in a room and write. I have to go out and have an experience.

Is the immediate feedback from an audience—which a writer doesn't get—another attraction of your speaking?

This lecturing is show business, and what I get is the feeling that I presume other performers get. What you're looking for is a conjunction of the speaker and the audience. Just this past weekend in Seattle, I had one of those occasions where the audience and I were *simpatico*. They were ahead of me. I didn't have to finish sentences. They knew what I was going to say, and I knew I could say almost anything. I could free-associate on stage. Those are great experiences.

Describe your typical road trip.

I'm going on the plane to these things, I'm keyed up, I'm psyched, I'm getting excited. I'm able to do a tremendous amount of work on the plane, usually correspondence. I feel like that all the way out.

Then comes the talk, then the depressing ride home, when I think of all the things I could have said. I relate every deficiency in the audience response to something that I have done.

Another thing about speaking is that I hate to repeat myself, and it's almost impossible to give a talk without repeating. So the worst thing that can happen is for someone to come up just before I'm going to speak and say, "I heard you last month in New Orleans" or somewhere. Here I'm going to say something as if it occurred to me for the first time, and he's going to know I'm faking it.

Do you follow the same outline in each talk?

No I don't. I never use any cues or notes. I occasionally write things on a blackboard, then never look at it. I have an opening and a closing planned, and I don't really know how things will go in between. I hope I'm going to get a whole fresh bag of ideas when I'm on stage. If the audience is good and I feel comfortable, I'll say many things that have been hidden away in my head and spontaneously pop up.

What helps me most is that I have to write a column every week. In getting my material together and thinking about it, I usually have enough material to write two or three columns. So I'm filled with these details and experiences. Whatever my column has been for the week somehow comes out in my talk—unless that column has been about blood in the urine. It's very difficult to introduce urine into a motivational talk.

You haven't mentioned yet what role your running plays in your writing and speaking.

As I say, I have maybe three columns worth of material, but it's straight information—disjointed thoughts which I've been writing down for three or four days, and that may have been in my head for months. I take the material with me out onto the road for an hour or an hour and a half, with the hope that during the run the one sentence that will set up the entire organization of the column will somehow come to me.

More often than not, it does. But I can't force it. I have to wait for it to come.

Lecturing happens almost the same way. I come into the town where I'm going to lecture in early afternoon. Then I'll go out and run for about an hour, trying to get some idea what I am going to say and some of the experiences to illustrate. There's no question that—whether you think anything on that run or you just come back completely confused—something happens to your physiology that puts you on stage in a relatively psyched yet relaxed mood. Very rarely have I failed in a talk after having run before.

In other words, you use your run as a warm-up exercise?

I do for a talk exactly what I do for a race. I don't eat, I warm up, I get psyched. Then I go out and do it. You can no more stroll out on a stage and give a talk than you can stroll up to a starting line and run a race. You've got to be prepared.

After about a thousand talks, why do you still get nervous before speaking?

Again it's like a race. I've run a thousand races too. If I don't get nervous, I'm going to bomb. I feel that completely. If I'm chatting with a friend and the gun goes off, I'm not prepared for the pain that is coming on right away. A reporter for a Houston paper said she saw me before one of my talks. She didn't think I would even be able to get to the stage, I was in such a state.

Right before a lecture is one of the few times I find I'm short with people. I very rarely have a harsh word for someone who says something nice to me or wants a book autographed. But if people come up while I'm getting into this kind of nervous storm that I need before I get on, I usually have to put them off. I regret this afterward, but that's one time when I really need privacy.

If you can shrink them to a few paragraphs, what are the current main themes of your speaking and writing?

What I say when I get up to talk is, "I'm not going to tell you anything you don't already know, but have forgotten. Mostly you've forgotten what it was like to be a child." We've forgotten about play. We've forgotten about our body. We've forgotten how good pain and discipline feel after we've used them. We've forgotten that we have a sense of humor.

These things are all inside. So I go before an audience to convince them that the body is important, that play is important, that discipline is important, that all these things involve a perspective toward what you're doing, which is what a sense of humor is—understanding the utter insignificance of whatever you do in life and the supreme importance of how you do it. That's what it comes down to.

Any writer with your visibility is bound to have critics. What kinds of criticism get under your skin?

First of all, the people who complain about what they feel is my excessive use of quotations. I don't think I use them excessively. I'm quite humble about my own capabilities. When I find somebody who said something better than I'll ever hope to, I've got to put it in. I'm not showing off my reading. My reading is not that extensive. When you look at these quotes, you find they're almost all from the same people. I read for the good sentence. I don't even care what the theme of the author's work is. Frequently I don't even know what the point of the whole work is. But I will find sentences that are memorable and that are the absolute right sequence of words to express a particular thought. A critic may say, "But that's out of context." It might be out of context for the writer, but it is the perfect context for me.

I do think that I have a lot lower opinion of book critics since my book was published. I think that, odd as it may seem, I have written a classic book.

Which book?

This ongoing book that I'm writing, which is now three books—*Dr. Sheehan on Running, Running & Being*, and *This Running Life*. This ongoing journal is a classic, maybe because we're dealing with a classic sport.

The reason it's a classic is that it is going to appeal over generations. I found that out because there are kids eight and ten years old reading it, and there are people seventy years old reading it. This book is going to be read long after the books that these critics applauded.

The thing I don't like about book critics is that they take it upon themselves to tell a reader not to read a book. I know of a specific instance where that happened with mine. A critic said, "If you have not read this book, don't waste your time reading it."

What are your own reading habits?

If someone suggests I read a new book, I go back and reread an old one. There are people who speak from one generation to another. It seems to me the writings that have survived for decades and even centuries are the ones to read. My reading is almost totally limited to acknowledged geniuses whose views and experiences of life correspond with mine. That's hard to come by.

Do you read running publications?

I don't. One reason is that I'm derivative enough, and I don't want to steal anything from any other running writer.

And good writing on my subject, running, makes me nervous. I don't want to read and then say, "God, that guy is good! How will I ever be able to top that?"

Are you still trying to top the work George Sheehan has done before?

I was at a meeting in Kansas City, talking to a group of directors of an association. I said I felt a good deal of empathy with everyone in the audience. I felt that what I had to say was important because all of us in that room were underachievers. Other people wouldn't think so, but we thought so.

That's the reason why at sixty-two I'm not sitting watching the ocean, which I could do. I've paid my dues. Lots of people my age are sitting in Florida now, but I feel I've never achieved what I could. I haven't run as fast as I can, I haven't spoken as well as I can, and I haven't written as well as I can. If you take less than that view, you're finished.

E S S A Y

DOC'S PLAYGROUND
BY ELLIOTT DENMAN

Be a good animal... The serious business of play... Meditations on racing... The road to revelation.

Are you kidding? Way Back When—the early 1960s, when Dr. George Sheehan was rediscovering the sport he'd abandoned since his Manhattan College days— metaphysics was never a factor in his personal exercise equation.

Truth be told, he really didn't give a hoot about the problems of being and reality—or the origin and structure of the universe, for that matter. All that came later, years later.

The Doc needed directions to a race—and the hot-off-the-mimeograph entry blank, if the race was elaborate enough to have such a thing—before he might ever ponder the road to revelation. He simply wanted to get in on the action, and Way Back When at the Jersey Shore, where the Brooklyn-born guy had been digging new roots for almost two decades, the only real action involved the high school kids.

The kids had this sport all to themselves then—until The Doc began crashing their party. At the drop of a high school schedule, he would descend on the turf of Christian Brothers Academy in Lincroft, the school he and other leaders of the community helped create. Or Long Branch High School, where a future Olympic steeplechaser named Bill Reilly was first revealed to the world. Or Red Bank Catholic High School, where Coach Jack Rafter, who'd go on to a remarkable three-decade run, had set up shop.

The high school kids and their coaches welcomed The Doc. He, after all, was the eccentric gent who kept insisting it was still possible for a man in—ohmygosh!—his forties to actually be a runner. And The Doc invariably repaid their hospitality by tripling up—running the freshman, junior varsity, and varsity races in order. The kids, in turn, kept wondering what kind of man this was who'd gasp his way to the finish line, and beat half of them.

A while later, The Doc's example began luring new friends to the running game. These were adult friends, full-growns, mostly ex-high school and college athletes who began to see that there might be life for them after graduation too. Having found "the road to revelation" in Rumson or Red Bank or Long Branch, Little Silver or Lincroft or Asbury Park, The Doc would go to work for the *Red Bank Daily Register* and then the *Asbury Park Press*— there to deliver the messages that would soon enough become the "meditations on racing" the whole world would embrace.

By the mid-1960s, the running game really began catching on—for far more than the kids—at the Jersey Shore. The Takanassee Lake Races, 5Ks on summer Monday nights, began in Long Branch and have raged on for thirty years under the guidance of the Shore Athletic Club.

The Doc loved Takanassee Lake. And Takanassee-goers got to love him.

When The Doc passed away, there would be just one place to hold the memorial services. Yes, St. Michael's Church at Takanassee Lake it would be. The running world would come to Doc's playground to say its most heartfelt goodbyes.

Plans are afoot to memorialize The Doc at Takanassee

Lake. The 5K runs will be named in his honor. A statue is on the drawing board. A foundation is being planned to keep all this going, for years and years and years. This "road to revelation" is just under eight-tenths of a mile around. Just under four laps equals 5K.

A few hundred of The Doc's favorite people will keep right on gathering here on summer Mondays. And the spirit of The Doc will surely hover over the place, forever and ever.

Elliott Denman, a veteran reporter for the Asbury Park Press, *competed in the 1956 Olympic Games as a 50-kilomter race walker.*

CHAPTER 7

EARLY WARNING

My many reunions with George Sheehan are usually joyous. Not this time. This meeting at the Bix Seven road race was our most somber, because a friend of ours had died unexpectedly and much too young the week before. This loss was more than personal. It rocked our sport and threatened to end the running boom.

The sport had boomed since the early 1970s and appeared on the brink of a new explosion of interest tied to the Olympic Games. They opened in Los Angeles this same weekend. The U.S. was home to the women's and men's world recordholders in the marathon, Joan Benoit and Alberto Salazar. They might have swept the gold medals at L.A.

Road racing had gone fully and openly professional in this country. George Sheehan remained as well known as any of the pro runners. George had sailed past his sixty-fifth birthday. Retired from his medical practice, he gave full attention to his running work. He raced, wrote, and spoke as well and as often as ever.

Now came the tragic news. As the leading spokesman for the sport, George was called on most to answer critics who almost gleefully pointed out the risk of running, and to reassure runners who now felt vulnerable.

"Exercise won't do what physicians think it will do," George said in his Davenport talk, answering the question on everyone's mind this week. "It will give you maximum performance and productivity out of your built-in longevity quotient, but I don't think it will extend it. Exercise offers performance—and that's what it's all about.

It has nothing to do with disease, and that's what we have to tell the truth about. That's what this death highlights.

"From this episode, it appears that it's not always safe to exercise. But you're only at risk if you exercise beyond your comfort range.

"If you follow your body, you'll train comfortably, humanely. Look, no horse ever ran itself to death without a jockey on its back. The trouble is, we're not intelligent enough animals."

§ § § § §

Running's three bestselling authors all came together in Dallas last December. Dr. Kenneth Cooper invited George Sheehan and Jim Fixx to speak at the White Rock Marathon and to visit Cooper's Aerobics Center for testing. The visiting writers both had an aversion to testing. Fixx had written in his *Complete Book of Running* about George advising him against taking unnecessary tests.

"Before setting out for Red Bank," Fixx recalled about his interview with George for the book, "I had made a bargain with my wife. Though I felt fine, for some time she had been prodding me to have a physical examination.

"I had told her that I'd not only ask Sheehan's advice, but would dutifully abide by whatever he recommended. Now I asked him what he thought a ten-mile-a-day runner with no troubling symptoms should do."

George's reply: "Annual physicals are a waste of time. You've got to listen to your body, and it isn't going to be replaced by machines. Stress tests, for example, are virtually useless in athletes—and they're not always very useful for other people.

"We do a stress test at a temperature of 70 degrees and 40-percent humidity. You haven't eaten in two hours, and there are a lot of nice people around. When you go out to run, it usually isn't anything like that."

George concluded, "All you're going to find out in an annual physical are things that you already know, or that are of no consequence to you." He talked Fixx out of taking a test that day in Red Bank. Seven years later in Dallas, when Dr. Cooper offered to measure Fixx's physical responses to exercise, he declined.

George accepted Cooper's offer. He jumped eagerly onto the treadmill but not to check for disease. This became a competitive event, as described in a subsequent column:

> Dr. Cooper, who was the first to turn the country toward aerobic exercise, has people come from all over the world for fitness testing. This particular week, he had a very fit and very distinguished visitor—Johnny Kelley, the seventy-six-year-old wonder from Cape Cod, who has run the last fifty-two Boston Marathons. He was undergoing a series of tests that would culminate in a try for the Cooper clinic treadmill record for seventy-and-overs.
>
> The word "record" set my juices flowing. I had just turned sixty-five and was ready to do battle in that age category. "Would it be possible for me to try for the sixty-five-and-over record?" I asked. Cooper immediately set an appointment for seven the next morning. The mark I had to shoot at, he told me, was 28:15—a time I associate with a race a little short of five miles.
>
> I felt insecure at first because I was not allowed my prerace coffee. I felt an additional insecurity as the grade of the treadmill increased steadily, one percent a minute. This was to be a hill test, and I am never at home on hills.
>
> At twenty-two minutes, Dr. Cooper informed me that I had just passed the elite in the fifty-and-over group. I gave a wave of my hand. "So long, guys," I said. A minute or so later, I left the elite forty-year-olds in my wake. Then, at twenty-five minutes, I forged ahead of the elite thirty-and-overs. I was now up with the best, regardless of age.
>
> Fifteen seconds away from the record, everything began to tighten up—my neck and chest, my arms and legs. But I knew nothing could stop me now. I had become pure willpower. My protesting body would just have to do it.
>
> Then I heard Cooper say, "Twenty-eight minutes, sixteen seconds—a new record." Suddenly I had nothing left. Whatever had propelled me that last minute was gone. When Cooper asked if I could make it to 28:30, I nodded yes but didn't do it.

Jim Fixx only observed this stress test. Seven months later, George asked himself what might have been discovered that day if he had insisted Fixx take his turn on the treadmill.

§ § § § §

The noon news on the car radio led off with the story: "The man who wrote the book on jogging has died while jogging..."

Two names flashed across my mind: George Sheehan and Kenneth Cooper.

"Fifty-two-year-old Jim Fixx..." The report went on with sketchy details about the heart attack that had killed Fixx while he vacationed in northern Vermont.

In those few seconds and the few minutes that followed, memories of Jim Fixx and emotions for him rushed to mind. I remembered first seeing his unfamiliar name on a letter in 1976. He wrote to say he was working on a book about running, and he wondered if we could get together and talk about it when he visited California. Soon after, a voice joined the name when Jim called to say he was in town—staying in a cheap motel along the fast-food strip—and could we meet? I put the name and face together with a person and a personality that day. This was the man who within two years would be starring on network talk shows and in "Do you know me?" ads.

At the time, he dressed in Levis cords, well-worn Tiger training flats and a T-shirt from an obscure race in New England. He truly looked like a runner—a fit one, younger than his forty-four years—not the chain-smoking, Type-A editor he had been nine years and sixty pounds earlier, and not a big-time writer trying to cash in on the burgeoning running craze. Only later did I learn that Fixx still was a prominent magazine editor in New York City. He mentioned his *Saturday Review, McCall's,* and *Horizon* credits casually and without embellishment. He'd put that work behind him for a while, taking a leave of absence to work on this book.

"It's a dream come true," he said, "a runner getting to spend a few months of total immersion in running. I was surprised when Random House gave me a big enough advance to let me take a few months off for this project." He said he never expected to earn anything more than that modest amount of upfront money for the yet-unnamed book. He meant that, and didn't seem to mind at all.

The Complete Book of Running came out a year later. It made Jim Fixx rich and famous beyond his imaginings. It seemed to put him on easy street, in a neighborhood where he would never have to work again. The trouble was, he wanted to keep working. He didn't want to let fame and fortune change his life. But they did anyway.

We met at Boston in 1978. He shook his head at all the fuss being made over him, and complained that writing this book about running had taken away his time to write and run. His time was never again completely his own. For the next six years, Jim Fixx lived a celebrity's life. He took a bemused view of it in his book *Jackpot*, but you could read some pain into those pages. He claimed to have slipped quietly back into obscurity after his books fell from the bestseller lists, but that wasn't true. Jim Fixx, a private man perfectly suited to the solitary existence of a writer/runner, remained a public figure who died a celebrity's death.

My first reaction to the news was shock, followed later by anger. Some reports suggested that the way Fixx died canceled out the way he had lived.

Running had killed this most famous of runners, or at least not protected him from heart disease as he said it should. Therefore all that he stood for in his writing must be untrue. Running must be unsafe.

Running didn't kill Fixx. Choosing the wrong father, a man who suffered his first heart attack at thirty-five and died in his early forties, might have shortened Jim's life (or running might have let him outlive his dad). His own early smoking and obesity may have left seeds of destruction in his coronary arteries (or running may have delayed the growth of those seeds). His refusal to take regular physical checkups or to heed danger signs in the last weeks could have brought him to this tragic end (or he could have died from complications of bypass surgery).

If Fixx could write this final chapter of his life story, he would find a light, self-effacing way of blaming himself for what happened. That was how he wrote.

He wouldn't blame the sport that made his life better, if not longer. He would advise other runners to pay more attention to the precautions he ignored, but not to let his mistakes harm running's good name.

Jim Fixx might end his story by saying that if he had to go too soon, let it be quickly and with his running shoes on.

§ § § §

George Sheehan felt compelled to write about the clinical details of his friend's death, to answer the concerns of runners everywhere.

What happened? "At autopsy, Fixx had severe coronary disease and evidence of an earlier nonfatal heart attack," George began. "Here is an instance of a dedicated high-mileage runner who collapsed and died, ignorant of the fact that he had serious heart disease.

Why did it happen? "He had an extremely bad family history. This is a highly significant risk factor. A study in Utah using the Mormon geneology tables showed that 50 percent of heart attacks occurred in 5 percent of the families."

What could have been done? "Fixx had warning. He told his fiancee that for several weeks he had been experiencing a tightness in his chest while running. My experience is that most people who suffer a heart attack or collapse suddenly have these warnings. Unfortunately, many people ignore them or, perhaps better said, *deny* them."

George Sheehan's concerns about heart disease were professional, not personal. "My family simply doesn't have heart problems," he told me in Davenport. "Something else will get me."

Later this same year, he would learn what that might be.

FOREVER YOUNG
BY GEORGE HIRSCH

George Sheehan and I go back to what is fondly known as the good old days. This was back when the term "running boom" was as unheard of as Diet Coke, computer dating, couch potato, MTV, or safe sex. Almost no one cared about running back then except for a small band of us. And we cared a lot.

In those days, the Boston Marathon was our Super Bowl, World Series, and Final Four combined. Boston was the center of our universe, and it always seemed to be George's mecca. Back then, we knew most of the field and got to chat with half of them in Hopkinton before the start. Everyone wanted to talk to George, usually to discuss some malady or another. He always had time—then and later, after running boomed along with his own popularity—for all the questions. He returned phone calls and answered letters from all over the country. In the weeks leading up to Boston, it seemed he did nothing else.

I'm not sure where he found time for his own training, but he was always at the starting line. After the marathon, he would put his thoughts in writing, and they always touched a nerve. George often wrote about the childlike feelings that came from running. Once, after a really hard ten-miler in Central Park, he and I were sprawled out on the floor of the Church of Heavenly Rest during the awards ceremony. George had easily won his age group.

"I feel like I just pulled the sword from the stone," he said. "This is one of those peak experiences." Then he added, "In fifth grade, we had peak experiences all the time." At his seventieth birthday party, he was asked what he wanted to be when he grew up. He replied, "A fifth grader again."

I remember an icy race one day in Central Park when I took a fall and landed hard. I walked back to the finish, and George said we should go to Lenox Hill Hospital for

X-rays. George said he'd speed up my trip through the emergency room. Three hours later, we were still sitting there—only to prove that a few blocks from the park, where George was a dazzling star, he was just another skinny Irishman. Finally we got the X-rays, and it was a broken shoulder. We picked up some painkillers, a dozen donuts, made coffee, and he, Mary Jane, and I sat in my house, talking well into the evening.

It was one of those delightful, all-too-infrequent days. You might call it a peak experience.

Over the years, I'd call George and ask him how he was doing. He always answered in numerical terms. "I ran 31:42 in Omaha on Sunday," he'd say, as if my question could only mean one thing. I remember once asking him about a mutual friend I hadn't seen in years. "What's he doing these days?" George answered, "Oh, about six a day."

That's the point. George is the truest runner of us all.

George Hirsch, publisher of Runner's World *magazine, spoke these sentiments at George Sheehan's April 1993 tribute dinner.*

P A R T   I I
MILES TO GO
(1986-1992)

C H A P T E R   8

DR. PATIENT

George Sheehan is a world-class worrier. He worries that he hasn't written well enough (though he has few peers as a running writer), spoken well enough (though no one on the running-clinic circuit speaks better), or run well enough (though he's one of the country's fastest men his age). George calls me regularly to say, "It's all over, I'm finished," in one of his three specialties. Then he comes right back to exceed himself.

So when he called to report "good news and bad news," I wasn't too worried. We'd been through this routine many times before.

The good news: "I've read through the manuscript again"—we're working on another book together, *Personal Best* for Rodale Press—"and I like it. But it needs a lot more work." I thought that was the bad news—heavy revision needing to be done. George went on to list changes that he wanted and I didn't want to make. We'd argued over them before, but this was an argument he would always win in the end. It was his book, not mine.

Just when he seemed ready to hang up the phone, he said, "Now I have something bad to tell you. I have a malignancy."

A doctor had found a growth on George's prostate. One had been discovered there two years ago, but dismissed as "benign."

"I think they goofed," George said. "It probably was there all along, and now there's no doubt about it. Prostate cancer is usually slow to develop and spread. And mine already has reached the Class-D stage, the most serious level. It has spread into my bones."

Speaking like a doctor talking about another patient, not himself, George outlined his immediate course of action:

"First comes a trip to Cleveland to see a doctor who's a whiz with this type of cancer. He'll probably call for surgery. When, I don't know—but surely it will be soon."

Then comes the waiting and wondering. How much has this disease progressed? How fast is it moving? How well can its advance be stalled?

"As it looks now," said George, "I have a very aggressive form of cancer. The two-year death rate is 85 percent." He said it that way rather than as a 15-percent chance of survival. This is in keeping with his tradition as a worrier, but it also reflects the medical realist who knows the odds don't favor him.

George's news brought me a rush of memories of words he'd spoken and written. He seemed to know early on that this would be his fate.

One of the earliest columns he sent me to edit talked about the "seventy-year warranty" issued to us at birth. He was in his fifties when he wrote this, and now he's little more than two years shy of seventy. This could be the age when his own warranty expires. Years ago, George wrote that heart disease didn't worry him at all. He's a cardiologist, and in no way does he fit the profile of his sick-hearted patients. He listed cancer as his biggest threat.

When Jim Fixx died in 1984 of a heart attack, George said, "That is a death to make your mouth water."

George wasn't being hard-hearted. Fixx was his friend and fellow author, and he grieved over the loss. He was saying that he'd much prefer a sudden, active, relatively painless death to the type he dreaded: a slow, debilitating, painful passing. Now the latter prospect faced him.

§ § § § §

In late 1984, George Sheehan got his first sign of trouble to come. He was in Dallas to speak at the White Rock Marathon, and while there visited Dr. Kenneth Cooper at the Aerobics Center.

Dr. Cooper couldn't pass up a chance to give George a complete physical exam. The year before, Fixx had gotten away without one that might have saved his life. Cooper wasn't going to let another of running's legends slip through his net.

"I was in Dallas to give a talk at a fitness festival," George wrote at the time in his newspaper column. "The day before, I had challenged Dr. Ken Cooper's treadmill and had broken the record for my age group. Afterward, as I lay on a table recovering, I felt as if I had joined the immortals. Despite my age, I had performed in the 99th percentile of the seventy thousand tests done at the Aerobics Center.

"That was when he discovered this suspicious area in my prostate. The news was paralyzing. I had just joined the immortals, and suddenly I was aware of my mortality."

He had the growth biopsied, then sweated out a week waiting for results. Before knowing how serious his condition might be, he concluded that "whether this nodule turned out to be benign or malignant, my life has been unalterably changed." After hearing a good report, he wrote, "The week of waiting has led me to the truth. Mortality is inevitable.

"This was no pardon I have received. It is a temporary stay. Eventually I will come to justice. I have been granted a little more time to deal with death."

George was given just sixteen months before he had to face the inevitable even more directly than before. The lines he wrote after the first lecture carry even more meaning now.

"In my lectures on fitness, I have always put down the argument that it extends life. Who among you, I ask, is concerned about longevity?

"I answer that question in the next breath. No one. What we are interested in is *performance*. Our consuming concern is getting up in the morning and doing our best the rest of the day."

Thinking about that answer later, George added, "But what is performance but pushing back death? It is our best rebuttal to mortality. Daily, by deed or subterfuge, we make our argument against the essential truth of the human condition."

§ § § § §

The day George Sheehan broke his dreadful news to me, I asked him if it was too personal or painful for him to make public. Without hesitating, George said, "No." I haven't said anything here that he wouldn't say even more openly.

"For a writer," he told me, repeating one of his favorite lines, "there are no bad experiences. There are just good stories." George will find the good stories in his experiences to come, and then he will keep no secrets. Nothing is too personal for a writer like him to make public.

"I have to write about it," he said. It's both a professional duty and a personal need. However his life story turns out, he must report it.

When his marriage broke up after almost forty years, he wrote about it without holding back any of the painful details. When an affair with a woman thirty years his junior ended, he aired his most private thoughts. After his first cancer scare, George told how he wanted to change in the extra time he'd been given. "At about the same time my problem surfaced," he wrote, "I heard a former United States Senator tell of his reaction on learning he had a malignancy.

"He had resigned from the Senate, but not for medical reasons. He could have finished his term satisfactorily. His reason for leaving was the heightened awareness this malignancy had given. He had reexamined his life and then determined to live it in a different way. He had discovered that there were people in his life more important to him than his position."

George made the same discovery in late 1984, and has acted on it since. "When you are between the sword and the stone," he wrote then, "you know whom you want standing beside you. When time becomes short, those who are essential to your life become obvious.

"The people who know they have cancer have their own motto: Make every day count. I have done that. What I have not done is make every *person* count.

"My life has been filled with the best of me. What it has not been filled with is the best of others."

The latest shock has brought home that truth even more urgently. George told me during his cancer-revealing call that he had broken off with a younger woman ("she didn't need a sixty-seven-year-old man, and definitely doesn't need one with cancer") and is planning to move back home to his long-time wife.

§ § § § §

George Sheehan never told me not to write about his disease. All he asked was, "Let me be the first to break the news. Then it's fair game."

The best-known running doctor felt little need to keep his condition secret. Yet he didn't want it written about in a way that might inspire pity that he wasn't seeking. The rumors spread anyway. We automatically think the worst when we hear this word "cancer," one of the most chilling in the language. The rumors greatly exaggerated George's current condition, placing him on the critical list. On hearing misinformation, I privately corrected it.

Meanwhile, he needed some time to plot a treatment course with his doctors. And to make whatever peace he could with the disease. George learned that while he has a serious illness, he is not now seriously ill. He feels few symptoms, and no radical treatments have been undertaken. He now knows that the metastasized cancer is beyond the reach of surgery. He has received no chemotherapy. He relies primarily on hormones to keep the cancer in check.

I saw George a few weeks after his announcement call.

He spoke in Medford, Oregon, and didn't miss a beat in his talk.

The greatest regrets he expressed to me then were being unable to run that weekend's Pear Blossom 20K—due to a calf injury, not the cancer—and the effect his news would have on others when he released it. While in Medford, George visited an athlete of similar age who had the same illness (and would soon die of it). George never mentioned his own condition to this man.

The reality of his own disease and its effects took several months to settle in. George then went public by way of an interview with Gerald Secor Couzens for *New York Newsday*.

"When I first got my diagnosis," he told Couzens, "I just gave up. I planned my will and turned down speaking engagements. I wasn't sure I'd be around in three months to fulfill any of them."

He also stopped writing and dropped out of racing. But he soon realized that waiting to die was no way to live whatever remaining time he had.

The first months of his new life passed. The disease stabilized, and George came to terms with it mentally. He'd learned to live with his cancer and to work through it. By the time of this interview, George had booked talks all the way into 1988. He'd also returned to a full menu of writing, running, and racing.

"When I go out to run," he said in the *Newsday* interview, "I don't run with the anticipation that it will do anything for my cancer. I do think there's a possibility that if I keep my immune system at a high level I may slow down the cancer's growth. I'm not sure that will happen, and I'm not counting on it. What I'm counting on when I run is the impact that cancer has on my life.

"If I didn't run and gave up to the cancer, became sedentary, then I'd lose everything that I have in my life. I run in order to remain as healthy as possible, regardless of what the disease does to me."

E S S A Y

DOCTOR'S DOCTOR

BY JOAN L. ULLYOT, MD

Like many runners I was injured rather frequently in my first running years. This was not surprising, in retrospect, since I was doing everything wrong—from lousy shoes to a misplaced emphasis on speed.

When rest and home cures didn't work, I limped off to the local orthopedist. Again, like many runners, about all I got was a head shake and a gloomy suggestion that I try some other, presumably less arduous, sport—like swimming.

"But I'm a *runner!*" I wailed, practically in tears. "Well, if you keep on running, you'll just fracture something else" was the lugubrious reply.

Then I found George Sheehan and was saved. Some friend introduced me to *Runner's World* magazine, and I devoured the "Medical Advice" column month after month. It was the first piece I turned to in each issue. This Dr. Sheehan had answers to all sorts of plaintive questions addressed to him by grounded runners. Victims of palpitations, heart murmurs, sciatica... Dr. Sheehan reassured them all.

A man of allegedly poor protoplasm, he confessed to having suffered most of the common ailments himself. He had gained a certain perspective about injuries, as well as the limitations of the medical profession.

Don't listen to nonrunning doctors, was his admonition. They have never studied the stresses and strains of the athletic body, nor are they aware of its healthy peculiarities. Listen to your body, use common sense, put inserts in your shoes, and keep on running.

Such advice reinforced my own inclinations and gave me the courage to explore remedies of my own. Injuries rarely occurred, and then only when I had done something excessively stupid. I had learned to carry on the proper dialogue with my body. Thanks to Sheehan's columns, my own running career prospered. He became the doctor whose opinions I valued most, the only one who *understood*.

Several years passed before I actually met him. His bestselling books, with his portraits on their covers, had not yet appeared and I had no idea what Sheehan looked like. I suppose I pictured him as a large, bluff (if lean) Irishman of the Boston mold—red of face and hearty of manner.

At a podiatric sports-medicine conference he was to speak at in 1974, I craned my neck for a view of the podium. I couldn't pick out the famous Dr. Sheehan. Finally a small, diffident man with thinning gray hair was introduced as the renowned MD. It's hard for me to recall my instant of shock, because I now know that Sheehan looks just the way he *should* look. After all, he now writes about his own appearance, not just medical problems. "I am the fox," he says of his body build. But for one expecting the lion, the fox came as a surprise intitially.

Sheehan's speech to the podiatrists was primarily concerned with the rather basic role of the foot in running, and the then-novel concept that you could treat knee, hip, and back pains by correcting footplant. This focus on the biomechanical causes of pain, rather than the affected joints higher up, was revolutionary in those days. Some podiatrists had been claiming success with the approach, but since their focus is *always* on the foot, they were suspected of bias. Sheehan was a respected MD and made other MDs listen.

Any faithful reader of Sheehan's column was familiar with the foot theme. But I had been unaware of the doctor's gifts as a speaker. He had the audience laughing uproariously. "The guy's a stand-up comic," gasped my neighbor, wiping tears from his eyes. His writing is often humorous but with a dry, slightly biting tone. In person, Sheehan adds flavor with his expressive voice and slightly apologetic look. Before an audience, he is truly in his element. The verbal Irish tradition seems even better suited to him than the written word.

After his talks, many runners who wouldn't bother writing a letter can't resist a chance to query the doctor personally about their own medical problems. Sheehan responds patiently and sensibly. He is easy to locate— right in the middle of the largest clump of people, almost hidden, sitting down on a step and dispensing advice.

When he emerges from the crowd at last, heading out on a run, he is usually again at the center of a group— those who want to get to know him on the run. Sheehan never seems to mind.

He enjoys talking. He has a large family and crowds seem familiar, even homey. Asked once if the hectic lecture schedule bothered him, if he didn't get tired of talking to runners, Sheehan smiled. "I loved it," he said. "I'm a ham."

Joan Ullyot, who wrote this piece in the late 1970s, became a running celebrity herself and often shared the speaking stage with fellow physician George Sheehan. She is the author of two books, Women's Running *and* Running Free.

CHAPTER 9

ROAD WORK

Everybody now knows. The word is out in a big way.

It went out to nearly half a million *Runner's World* subscribers when George Sheehan made the announcement in his return-to-the-magazine column. George had left *RW* in the early 1980s to write for *The Runner*. Now the two magazines had combined under Rodale Press ownership and the *Runner's World* logo.

In his May column, George's first since the merger, he wrote, "Psychologist Abraham Maslow called the years subsequent to his heart attack his 'postmortem life.' It was a time he viewed as a gift—hours of appreciating what he had taken for granted, days used in the best possible way."

George explained that in medicine "postmortems are done to ascertain the cause of death." He said that for the living who've had a health scare or just need a change of direction "a postmortem life should uncover what was wrong with the previous one.

"Each New Year's Day, we think on failures in the past and make resolutions about the future. What has happened to me has made this traditional practice tremendously important. I see clearly that my life depends on what I decide to do with it." He talked mainly about giving the people around him a larger role in his life. But he also spoke of work yet to be done.

George ended his May 1987 *Runner's World* column by writing, "I now know that Robert Frost was right. I have promises to keep, and miles to go before I sleep."

He went back on the road to travel those miles and honor those promises.

§ § § §

Runner's World sent a feature writer, John Brant, to
follow George Sheehan's speaking trail around the West
this summer. The resulting story is the best description
ever written of George in action. Here is a portion of
Brant's report, which begins in San Diego:

Twenty minutes until showtime, and George Sheehan
is stalking. He's treading the plush-piled lobby between the
coffee service and registration desk, his head down, his lips
pursed, his fine-boned hands stroking his chin. He's wearing a blue oxford shirt and seasoned jeans, a ratty pair of
dishwater-colored anklets and an unspeakable pair of
walking shoes. His skin is sallow, his shoulders hunched.
All in all, Sheehan looks as bad as anyone knowing his
condition might have feared.

But there's purpose behind Sheehan's stalk, and a
shrouded strength. Like Ralph Waldo Emerson, one of his
idols, he's searching for a good sentence. When he finds it,
he'll begin his transformation. Once in front of his audience, he'll puff and swell, his skin will glow, and his eyes
will gleam. His movements about the stage will seem both
restless and sure, resembling far more a panther on the
prowl than a man nearing seventy.

Unconsciously, Sheehan will be acting out another of
his favorite Emersonian edicts: First be a good animal.

The audience consists of physicians gathered in San
Diego for a sports-medicine conference. But the scene
seems more timeless than particular. For hasn't Sheehan
always been with us? The suburban cardiologist from Red
Bank, New Jersey. The proselytizing distance runner. The
counterpunching popular philosopher of aerobic exercise.

When he's introduced, there's an expectant scrape and
rustle of paper, chairs, and water glasses. Then he's striding
up to the stage—unaccompanied by applause, according
to medical-meeting protocol.

Sheehan seizes the microphone and, ignoring the lec-
tern, begins pacing about the stage, sizing up and seducing
his audience. Listening to Sheehan, like listening to a good
stand-up comedian, is a matter of being let into a carefully
edited stream of consciousness. His purpose is to impart
the seemingly old but still welcome news that fitness can
and should be intrinsic to everybody's life.

Moreover, by Sheehan's lights, fitness should not be practiced simply for usefulness, but toward some larger, more generous, and more fundamental conception of physical and mental health. "Fifty, a hundred years ago it was 'be good,'" Sheehan says to the doctors. "Now it's 'be happy.'"

And what Sheehan tells us so entertainingly, in his pleasing yeasty Brooklyn accent, is that through running and thinking we can—we are compelled to—achieve both. In motion lie both happiness and goodness.

The doctors chuckle, dropping down their professional guard. They realize they are going to enjoy this.

Then Sheehan lights up his overhead projections, hand-printed and almost touchingly crude compared to the shiny full-color charts and prints of his colleagues. As much as possible, he lives a life unfazed by technology.

A few hours earlier, in the hotel men's room, Sheehan raised more than a few eyebrows by stripping down to shave. When he discovered he'd forgotten his shaving cream, he lathered up with hand soap from the dispenser.

Sheehan leaves the podium amid a dense rain of applause. About a dozen members of the audience close around him with questions and comments. Sheehan suffers them patiently, still responding with quotes and parables. When the crowd disperses, he wanders out to the lobby in search of coffee.

His second talk, beginning an hour later, is concerned with the poetry of running rather than its science. Sheehan has always believed that running is sport first and foremost, and good medicine a distant second. He didn't start running for his health, rarely used running in his cardiology practice, and doesn't recommend running to heart patients. He agrees that, for most people, walking is sufficient and safe.

The speech ends to another respectful round of applause, and again the knot of questioners, the curious and the proselytizers, gather around. Sheehan furrows his brow, opens himself up to them, yet at the same time keeps his distance.

Or perhaps it's that the spectators instinctively keep *their* distance. There's something formal and stern—a brooding quality—about Sheehan, no matter how outwardly agreeable he makes himself. A few people ask about his running or invite him to a race or workout. Everybody assumes he runs more than he does.

"I don't usually run when I'm on the road," he admits. "I nap instead."

§ § § § §

Once in a great while, George Sheehan even gets to come home to work as a speaker. One of the country's finest 10-kilometer races starts within a mile of his oceanfront home in New Jersey. He can go out his front door in Ocean Grove, cross the street to the boardwalk, turn left and take a warmup run to the starting line of the Asbury Park Classic. After the race, George can gather his friends for a cooldown run and an afternoon of recovering and celebrating on his deck.

George thought this year's Asbury Park 10K would give him problems, though. His racing pace had fallen off dramatically since he went on hormone therapy for his cancer. He usually relishes the give and take of question-answer sessions after his talk. But the night before this race, someone asked a question that stabbed at his heart.

"How does it feel to be setting personal worsts every time you run?" this listener wanted to know. George's answer: "Embarrassing." He complained that his all-out pace is now slower than he ran last year in training.

He added, "It also can be annoying when people in the trailing edge of a race pack ask me, 'What are you doing back here, Doc?' My first impulse is to say something about what can a runner on drugs for cancer expect."

Embarrassment and annoyance didn't keep George from running his hometown race. Afterward he wrote in his weekly column that his slower pace had taught him an important lesson. He began by repeating one of his pet themes: "There are no bad experiences." To his astonishment, "Running back in the pack at Asbury Park was enlightening and inspiring.

"I had always *written* as a representative of the also-rans. But in truth I was always an elite runner, one of the winners. I rarely came home from a race without a trophy, and more often than not was a winner in my age group."

George met runners who were new to him. He liked what he learned from them.

"What I discovered at Asbury Park was that, from leader to last man, the runners were running at the fastest pace they could. The eight-minute milers, for example, were taking no prisoners. They were not—as I once suspected—lollygagging along, engaged in conversation about last night's pasta party.

"They may not have the maximum oxygen capacity of those averaging two or even three minutes a mile faster, but it was costing them the same effort. They were paying with an equal amount of pain. And for me, gaining ground in this flow was just as difficult as it had been a year or so back at a much faster pace."

George discovered he was not the least bit embarrassed to be seen in the company of these eight-minute milers. He wrote, "Running back in the pack was an experience that affirmed that all runners are indeed equal. Only their times are different.

"Talent may separate us in a race. But I like to remind myself and my running friends once more of what William James said: that effort is the measure of a man.

"The eight-minute-mile club passes that test. And so will the ten-minute-mile club when I join it."

§ § § § §

John Brant, the *Runner's World* writer, picked up George Sheehan's travel trail again in September. An event in San Francisco provided this ending to Brant's fine article:

> Sheehan kept up his furious travels all summer. Colorado, Las Vegas, San Diego again, Los Angeles, and, in mid-September, San Francisco to address the annual meeting of the American Academy of Family Physicians. He looked better than he had earlier in the summer—fresher, stronger, calmer.
>
> The doctors requested his number-one speech—the science of exercise—and Sheehan responded with a bravura performance. He spoke in the main auditorium

of the vast Moscone Center but succeeded in making the space seem as intimate as a coffeehouse.

Afterward the usual knot of admirers formed around him. About two dozen people this time, and knowledgeable about his career and condition. Questions came about the cancer. Sheehan didn't dodge them, but he hardly celebrated them, either. He sketched in quickly how the disease had been discovered, but sidestepped one question about whether he might raise public awareness about cancer in the way that Jim Fixx's death had done for heart disease. The doctor had no interest in martyrdom.

After the crowd melted away, only two people remained. A married couple from Phoenix had flown in expressly to have dinner with Sheehan. The trip and dinner formed a birthday gift from the wife to the husband who, like many other runners, had hung on Sheehan's words for years.

There wasn't much time before they would all have to drive back to the airport. Sheehan was clearly moved— and a shade embarrassed—at the depth of his hosts' devotion. He tried to put them at ease, deflecting the conversation away from himself.

The couple was shy and more than a trifle starstruck. Here they were in San Francisco, eating dinner with Dr. George Sheehan. The husband, particularly, struggled not to stare.

"You're so much more personable than I expected," the man blurted and then stared down at his plate in embarrassment. The corners of Sheehan's mouth turned up briefly, then flattened. He looked down, too.

A dozen quotations might have come to mind. But Sheehan said nothing, letting his own silence speak for him.

E S S A Y

ON CALL
BY JIM FIXX

I had not been involved with running long before I learned who George Sheehan was and in what high regard he was held. When I started racing, I occasionally caught glimpses of him in Central Park, in Van Cortlandt Park, at various races in New Jersey and Connecticut, and two or three times in Boston.

He was a fragile-looking ragamuffin of a man who wore some of the most unprepossessing running clothes I had ever seen. On such occasions, we would nod and say hello, but we barely knew each other.

Finally, when I started work on my book, I decided it was time to make a pilgrimage to Red Bank and spend some time with him. I met Sheehan at Riverview Hospital, where he is director of the ECG department. Wearing an old pair of Tiger running shoes, he led me to the cafeteria to have a look at the Navesink River flowing past the hospital's windows. Far out the water was blue, and sailboats skidded back and forth on their moorings.

"There is a ten-foot tide out there," Sheehan said. "They have regattas and everything. Isn't it beautiful?" It was.

In the medical library, we sat down to talk. But from time to time the phone rang, and Sheehan would speak with a runner. One called from somewhere in the Midwest. After listening and advising, he pushed his chair back and put his feet up on a table.

"I get three or four of those calls a day," he said. "Unfortunately, the people who know anything about treating runners are few and far between.

"It's all right if you live on the West Coast, and we also have some pretty good guys in the East. But in the middle of the country, you run into all kinds of problems. Most runners get so they don't want to see anybody in any specialty unless he's a runner."

Sheehan said he had once hoped to educate doctors

about running but has all but given up. "These days," he went on, "I try to publish pieces where they'll be seen by athletes. I've found that our success in getting treatment for runners is proportional to how well we reach *them*, not to how well we reach doctors."

Whatever other doctors think of the Sheehan system of medical education, runners clearly like it and feel flattered by it. I asked what he thought accounted for the appeal of his writing.

"I don't understand it," he answered. "These little old ladies in Maintenance and Dietary are always coming up to me here at the hospital and saying, 'I love your book.' Once one of them stopped me in the corridor and said, 'Now how do you handle heat, Doctor?'"

Although Sheehan knows his writing has a special appeal for runners, he doesn't dwell on his accomplishments. "It's funny about my writing," he said. "I never expect to write another decent column. I'm reaching over my head every time. I said once that I felt like a .230 hitter waiting for someone to come along and do it really well. It's just that no one else has come along yet."

Excerpted from The Complete Book of Running, *Copyright © by James F. Fixx. Reprinted by permission of Random House, Inc. The book stood atop the bestseller list for most of 1977–78. Jim Fixx died in 1984.*

CHAPTER 10

CHANGING TIMES

Almost a year has passed since my last meeting with George Sheehan. We were together now at this seaside resort to help launch a series of masters races, limited to runners forty and older.

Giving George a welcoming hug, I felt a layer of padding around his middle that wasn't there before. It wasn't a bad sign to see a cancer patient gaining weight, and I assumed that his hormone therapy caused it. I didn't mention this to him, or the fact that he looked good. "Whenever anyone tells you you're looking good," he has said, "it means you're overweight and out of shape."

We passed through the buffet line together. I noticed he only took fruits and vegetables and guessed he was trying to shake those extra pounds. "You passed up all the goodies," I said of the sweet and fatty treats.

"I'm finally cleaning up my diet act," he answered. This was a man I had often watched eat bacon-and-egg breakfasts and cheeseburger-with-fries dinners.

"Dietary agnostic" is how George once described himself. He said then that arguing diets with runners "is like debating religion with a true believer." Both subjects offer much room for interpretation and opinion, but few absolute answers. George wanted little part of this debate.

He tells of an exchange after one of his lectures. The first question dealt with diet.

"I don't have much to say about it," he answered. The questioner reminded him that he'd been billed as saying a few words about diet.

"I just did," said George. "Next question."

But the subject couldn't be dismissed this easily. In response to aging, his illness, and mounting evidence that certain dietary changes do make a difference, George has softened his agnostic stance. He denies becoming a true believer. But this subject plays a growing role in his writing and speaking.

§ § § §

A Sheehan column reported his dietary change of heart. He realized its extent while flying out of Newark, New Jersey, on his way to Missoula, Montana.

"Once underway, breakfast was served," he wrote. "I looked down at my tray: cheese omelet, sausages, biscuit, and two pats of butter."

George asked for skim milk with his coffee. "Sorry," the flight attendant told him, "we're out." She gave him a choice between a fat-laden nondairy creamer and whole milk.

"I did the best I could. I scraped the cheese out of the omelet, dodged the sausages and biscuit and butter, then used just enough milk to lighten my coffee."

George changed planes in Minneapolis. The new flight brought a replay of the fatty breakfast. "This time, I refused," he recalled.

Asked to fill out a questionnaire on the airline's services, he wrote, "Within a space of three hours, I was given two high-risk meals."

He later related in his column, "Those of us who have taken the importance of blood-cholesterol levels to heart find it extremely difficult to avoid high-risk meals. The person who eats out a good deal is hard put to keep dietary fat low. Fat is ubiquitous."

Before George became fat-phobic, he often ate with a friend who already was. She would study a menu, no matter how long, and conclude, "There's nothing I can eat here."

"I thought then she was out of her mind," George wrote. "Now I know she was ahead of her time. There was not much to eat then, and there is not much more now.

"Constant vigilance is necessary. You must be prepared to go hungry, irritate your waiter, or even complain to the management. But it was like that in the past for nonsmokers. When they began to complain, they got results. Now restaurants have smoke-free areas. In time, they will have low-fat menus, too."

During one recent period, two of George's *Runner's World* columns within four months tackled diet topics. When Rodale Press wanted to see a sample chapter from his next book, George sent one on diet matters. The publisher asked that this chapter be no more than ten thousand words. George wrote more than that length and had enough material left over to do a whole book on diet. A three-hundred-word sampling reflects the extent of his conversion:

• On American eating: "Health has many enemies, but in the United States one of our major foes is the food we eat. From the health standpoint, the ordinary American diet is atrocious."

• On healthy eating: "Health and longevity depend on eating only what is necessary to sustain life—the less the better. The diet that comes with the affluent life is the killer. When we study long-lived people, we find that they eat only when hungry and no more than is needed."

• On high-fat eating: "My concern over this risk has grown in recent years. I now see that running alone doesn't cancel it out."

• On fatty foods: "It is time to declare war on fat. Fat is our enemy, yet fat in one form or another dominates our food supply. Menus, supermarket shelves, and snack-food dispensers are land-mined and booby-trapped."

• On high-carbohydrate eating: "Runners may be unaware that a normal diet is usually not sufficient to replace glycogen used in training. Carbo-loading, therefore, is not something to be reserved for the night before a race. It has to be done on a regular basis to maintain the body's glycogen reserves."

• On food intolerances: "It is quite likely that many minor deviations from feeling alive and healthy are due to foods and what is put in them. When we are just not up to par physically, mentally, emotionally, and socially, it may indeed be due to something we ate."

• On weight control: "The overweight person is faced with three choices: 1. be fat; 2. be hungry; 3. exercise. The first choice is unacceptable. The second choice is ineffective. Fortuntely the third alternative does work. Exercise is the rational, scientific, and successful way to lose weight."

• On running and eating: "Dieters look on food as the enemy. Runners look on food as their friend. While dieters are engaged in a hand-to-hand fight against food, runners are eating to their heart's content."

That is, if their foods are high in carbos and low in fat. As George's now are.

§ § § § §

George Sheehan doesn't just eat differently than he did before. His athletic menu has also changed.

He swam and bicycled when the pains in his legs wouldn't allow him to run. The running returned, and the other two activities remained. All three inevitably combined to turn this inveterate competitor into a triathlete.

This represented another great leap in his thinking. He wrote recently, "When people used to ask me why I didn't do triathlons, I had a ready answer: Swimming is boring, and cycling is dangerous.

"Eventually I became a triathlete by chance, as a way of filling these downtimes. I remain a triathlete by *choice*. I now swim, bike, or run for training, and I combine the three in triathlon races. My new program minimizes injuries (or at least their disruption of my life). Compared to running, swimming and cycling produce few overuse injuries, and when I can't run I can usually continue to work out in the water or on wheels."

George described a triathlon race in his home area. It started with an 800-meter swim, continued with twenty kilometers by bicycle, and ended with a 10K run.

"It was worse than anything I had imagined," he said of this race. "The swim was an absolute horror. One lifeguard on a surfboard kept asking me every few minutes, 'Do you need any help?'" On to the bike portion. "In short order, I was lapped by people who were six miles ahead of me."

He started the running segment just as the race winner was finishing his to the cheers of the crowd. George had planned to quit after two-thirds of the race. But the cheering did it. "I was ashamed to stop. I got off the bike and ordered my body to start running.

"And two hours and twenty-two minutes after I had entered the water, I finished. As I stood there watching the last of the winners cross the line, I thought, I've finally learned how to play this game."

§ § § § §

"How is George Sheehan doing?" The question comes up everywhere I travel and in almost every call at home. George is the sport's most revered writer and speaker, and he ranks in name recognition beside Olympic champions and world recordholders.

Concern for his health is as widespread as his fame. When he released the news in his *Runner's World* column a year ago, his prognosis wasn't good. Much has happened since. At first, he chose simply to wait until the condition worsened noticeably before deciding on the treatment course to take. By last spring, he was experiencing severe pain in his hips and legs. He began treatment.

The weeks that followed were his roughest since the

initial diagnosis in 1986. He hurt too much to run for six weeks, but his runner background sustained him.

"I don't think I could have gotten through that if I weren't a marathoner," he now tells Michael Hill of the *Baltimore Sun*. "In a marathon, you just sort of take whatever you're given. If there's a hill, you climb it no matter how much it hurts. That's the attitude I needed."

Michael Hill's article traces George's progress from the time he resumed running last summer. "When I started back," he says, "it was very difficult to enjoy it. It was hard for several weeks. But when I got back to enjoying my running, that was pivotal. I got control of my life again."

Part of that control was learning to talk openly, even humorously at times, about his condition. He now tells his audiences, "I take this medication that stops the body from producing testosterone [a male sex hormone]. I have less testosterone than the female runners do. I should be competing in the eunuch category."

George tells writer Hill, "Life has been described as a play with a lousy third act." The way to deal with it "is not by changing the plot—that's inevitable—but by changing the characters. And running and fitness do something about your character."

Sheehan says all his tests since he started running again have been encouraging. The cancer hasn't gone away, but it is under control. He says his fitness "has reduced the effect of the disease to virtually zero. It is only at maximum effort that I can tell any difference between myself before and myself after."

George doesn't run as fast as he did before, and he realizes he may never again see sub-seven-minute mile pace in a 10-kilometer race. But he's still trying to do his best under the circumstances, and he has improved his performances steadily since hitting bottom last summer.

Sheehan came out of treatment barely able to hold a nine-minute pace. He notes proudly that "every 10K has been faster since I've started back—56 minutes, 54 minutes, 51 minutes..."

How is George Sheehan doing? Better all the time, I'm

happy to tell everyone now asking about him. He looks good and feels good. He's eating better than ever before, training more completely than at any time in his adult life, and racing faster than he has in years.

At a Baltimore 10K race this spring, the occasion of Michael Hill's interview, George broke forty-eight minutes. If asked how he's doing, he might have said, "About 7:45 per mile." Instead he said, "I feel I've been reborn."

E S S A Y
SHEEHAN MOMENTS
BY JOHN BRANT

Some runners have private Sheehan moments, even without having experienced the man in person. Maybe it was 1977 and you were fresh out of school, trying to scratch out a start in some new and unyielding city.

Weary, luckless, you stumbled to a newsstand, where you picked up a copy of *Runner's World*. You turned to Sheehan's column, seeking some link back to those clean, electric days when you first started running. That month, Sheehan was writing about bursting into spontaneous tears of thanks as he ran his river route one afternoon. During the few minutes it took to read the column, you forgot about your confusions and footlessness.

When you were finished reading, you put the magazine back on the rack. You rubbed your hands up and down the legs of your jeans. Then you broke out of the store and back to your rented room. You changed as fast as you could and took off running. You were no longer lost. Sheehan had reminded you that your life was pinned to something. He had granted you solace and permission.

Therein lies the glory of Sheehan. His has always been a prose of conceit and near-excess—his column, even in the early days, teetering on the edge of self-parody. And yet, no matter what its flaws, his writing has always remained compelling. Perhaps it's his elevated, epigrammatic style or his unabashed love for neglected classical writers. Certainly it's the ardor and snap he brings to his work, the air that he's producing something durable and necessary—literature as much as journalism. At his best, Sheehan connects our running to something greater—something outside ourselves.

Like the sport he professes, Sheehan has grown both more popular and more maligned in recent years. As the boom swelled and subsided, a lot of people kept running but stopped talking about it so much—particularly in the terms that Sheehan kept insisting upon: self-knowledge, extending the limits, testing the mettle.

He remained a valuable and respected source of medical advice. But his more speculative writing and speaking, the work closest to his heart, became construed by some as tiresome and repetitive. It appeared that running was passing into a dowdy middle age and that Sheehan, the sport's soul and chronicler, was ossifying alongside it.

Then as he went public with his prostate cancer, his career was undergoing a subtle but unmistakable revival. He threw himself back into his work, writing compulsively, leap-frogging around the nation, spreading his word to whomever would hear it.

The competitive thrust that had him hammering sub-five-minute miles through his fifties was the same engine that drove his writing and fueled his curiosity about the world. Running and racing provided his metaphor. Using running as a tool, Sheehan still maintains, people can come to live their own lives, think their own thoughts, come to their own conclusions about how to live as women and men, animals and thinkers. He believes that running's chief contribution might be the solitary hour it gives most of its practitioners—"the hour of the oracles," he calls it.

He's a fierce proponent of the human capacity for transformation. His idealism is deeply but humbly rooted: "I don't think you can change yourself without changing your body."

Transformation, hours with the oracles, the wisdom of the body, heart, and mind. Intoxicating, nourishing stuff, and to varying degrees millions of runners have come to depend on George Sheehan for their supply.

John Brant is a senior writer for Runner's World *magazine. He wrote this essay in 1988 as part of an* RW *article.*

PERSONAL BEST

Still more changes. In response to lagging endurance, George Sheehan has reduced his running distances.

In writing, he attributes the drop in stamina to age and leaves it at that so as not to sound like he's making excuses for training less and racing shorter. But privately, he knows that his testosterone-blocking therapy is to blame.

"I've come face to face with a harsh reality—a severe drop in performance," he wrote earlier this year. "At seventy, I am no longer the runner I was only a few years back.

"'The longer the race, the older I feel. So I have taken that fact and come up with a logical corollary: The shorter the race, the *younger* I will feel. The solution is to begin at the beginning, to return to what I did as a boy and become the runner I first was—a sprinter. Perhaps age, which had sapped my stamina, has left me with some speed and sufficient strength from my youth to make it last for a minute or two."

The old road warrior switched to 100-, 200- and 400-meter dashes. In one track meet, George competed against an eighty-one-year-old and a seventy-six-year-old, lost to both, and didn't even mind.

He said, "These races are great fun—the competence, the sensation of speed, the expending of total effort, the quick recovery. In less than two minutes, I experience all the rewards of a five-mile race—with few of the drawbacks. Only in the final fifty yards do I feel the type of discomfort that predominates in most of the road races I enter."

George found that his current condition still allows him to run fast, just not for long. "My loss of speed is indeed less than my loss in stamina. On the track, I feel as fast as in my youth. But more than that, I feel at home."

He concluded, "It's appropriate that both the young, who have all the time in the world, and the aged, who no longer have enough time, both turn to the sprints. There, time is compressed into an unforgettable moment.

"Old age, which appears to be a matter of survival (and therefore endurance), is not that at all. Time, not distance, becomes important. Life is no longer a marathon. It becomes a 100-meter dash."

§ § § § §

Which is how George Sheehan happened to enter The World Veterans Championships for men over forty and women thirty-five and up. It's the closest an older runner can come to competing in the Olympic Games. World Vets meets are run every other year, but they never fit with George's competitive interests before. This is primarily a track meet, and he'd quit running track races before the first of these championships in 1975.

Now he was a trackman again. He signed up for the meet in Eugene, the track capital of the Western Hemisphere as well as my hometown.

This was the greatest event I've ever seen. And I've seen a lot in twenty-five years of covering this sport. The size and spirit of this meet moved me as no other has, including three Olympics.

Competition for veterans—or "masters," as older American runners call themselves—is still a young movement. The World Veterans Championships, which came to the U.S. for the first time this year, are only fourteen years old. Like a child of that age, vets running is both growing and maturing quickly. We're just beginning to see what its adult identity might be. In its short life, this arena has already produced three generations of winners. First came the new or renewed athletes.

These people (George Sheehan was one of them) who hadn't competed since their youth, if then, started training for fitness as adults and couldn't stop with that. They created the first demand for separate veterans' meets, and won most of the early prizes. The new opportunities for masters gave long-time runners in their thirties a new reason to continue. Soon a second generation of winning vets was born—formerly near-great athletes who won by outlasting the people who had outrun them in their youth.

Now the third generation is emerging—superstars who remained competitive until they reached vet status. The quality of competition has improved vastly because of them. So has the quantity of competitors. The WVC has more than tripled in size, to almost six thousand now, since its first edition at Toronto. But while growing bigger and better, these championships haven't forgotten their original purpose—to serve the athletes, not the interests of nations or fans.

Vets enter the Worlds as individuals, not as national teams. The individuals pay for their own trips. This meet makes room for anyone who wants to compete, no matter how unwieldy the program grows. No one is turned away because of advanced age, lack of ability or overcrowded fields. The officials simply add more age groups and races as demand warrants. The medal-winners, recordsetters, and superstars aren't the biggest news here. The top story concerns all these people who came to Oregon to compete—not to win, in most cases, but (in the best George Sheehan spirit) to do whatever their abilities will allow.

As the World Veterans Championships have grown, they've stayed truer to the original Olympic ideal than the Olympics have. The glory of the World Vets isn't reserved for the athletes who place first but extends to everyone who takes part.

Mr. Olympics himself, four-time discus gold medalist Al Oerter, competed in Eugene. He said later, "I truly enjoyed it. This is what the Baron [de Coubertin] had in mind when he started the Olympic movement way back when.

"This is more like the Olympics than the Olympics. It's the spirit of participation."

One of most emotional moments I've experienced in

sports came during opening ceremonies for the World Veterans Championships. I stood in a packed stadium as thousands of athletes marched in an Olympic-style parade.

"These are the elite of the planet," commented my wife Barbara. She isn't particularly a sports fan and wasn't speaking in athletic terms. These people from all over the world have lived through wars, and in some cases fought them against each other. They have lived through depressions and now prospered well enough to pay their own way here.

They have remained fit or reclaimed their fitness. They have been lucky enough to avoid accident and disease, or strong enough to overcome them.

§ § § § §

George Sheehan ranked as one of the world's elite, even before his World Vets race was run. He chose not to try the shortest sprints, but to run eight hundred meters, two laps around the track.

Hal Higdon covered the meet for *Runner's World* magazine. He called the 800 "the ideal race for these age groups. It's long enough to be tactical but short enough so no one gets lapped."

I watched the 800-meter finals with Matti Hannus, a Finn, and one of Europe's best-known running writers. He has run 800s for twenty-five years, but had one of his most disappointing days in the qualifying round here and talked then about abandoning the event. We stood for two hours as women and men worked down in age and up in speed at this distance. When this thrilling evening of racing ended, Matti said, "Now I know why I'll never leave the 800."

Alan Bonney, a college and club coach from Seattle, later wrote, "I've been a spectator at four Olympic Trials, at World Championships [for young athletes], and the Los Angeles Olympics. But none of those experiences measured up to what I witness in the World Veterans Championships."

Bonney's excitement peaked during the 800s, "where race after race brought tears to my eyes and joy to my heart. As the sections rolled on, one thing became clear: The athletes weren't as fast as they once were, but they were still athletic and competitive."

He added, "Perhaps Ponce de Leon was looking for the Fountain of Youth in all the wrong places."

George Sheehan had come full circle. He'd returned to the event of his youth after more than fifty years.

§ § § § §

George is a better runner in his seventies than he was in his teens. He has found a way to roll back the clock that tries to tell him he's slowing with age. Let him tell the story in a column that took shape as he flew home from Eugene. It might be the finest description of a race he ever wrote:

> It was early evening in Eugene, and the lights were on at Hayward Field. In the grandstand, five thousand people watched the World Veterans Championships, still buzzing over the previous race as our group of eight was led to the starting line for the men's 70-74 800-meter final.
>
> Months ago, these championships—short distances, run on the track—were of little interest to me. Over the years, my passion had been road races of five miles or more. I was a track runner and had long since lost any desire to run on the track. But age and time are not congenial to maintaining the status quo. They do not permit an everlasting present. There are cycles to our life, just as in all of nature. The winter of the seventy-year-old yields to the spring of the adolescent.
>
> When I began running at Brooklyn Prep, I ran the half-mile. My running was limited to a few minutes of fear, followed by effort, then pain, and then peace. The youthful middle-distance runner knows full well that the 800-meter race is an inextricable mix of joy and pain.
>
> At seventy, I returned to the body and play and wisdom of that teenager. I returned to the races of my youth.
>
> Instead of getting old, I became young, and in Eugene I was the adolescent living the adolescent's dream. I was in Hayward Field, the mecca of track and field, filled

with people. The floodlights glistened on the red track, still wet from an earlier rain. The infield was an incredible, improbable emerald green. The whole scene had an Olympic quality. The finalists included four Americans, an Australian, a New Zealander, a German, and a Swede. I could hear the announcer introducing each of us by name, country, the lane we occupied, and our achievements. Then I heard the starter say, "Runners, set!" The gun sounded, and I was running the World Championship 800-meter race.

It was enough to make anyone lose his wits, and I did. I had gotten in the final by going out slowly in my qualifying heat and picking off four runners with a fast last lap. I had planned a repeat of this strategy, but this time the world's best 800-meter runners went out at flank speed, and I went with them. With four hundred meters to go, I felt like I was finished, but I held on to pass the German and finish seventh.

I tore my hamstring during the race, but it was worth it. I was an adolescent living an adolescent's dream.

Afterward as I sat on the box with the big "8" indicating my lane, an official came up and said I had run 2:48.2. A personal best on a personal-best evening. As I walked to the far side of the field, the men's 65–69 800-meter qualifiers passed me, bound for a like experience. Eight more adolescents entering their field of dreams.

Later, when I was flying home, still filled with this sense of being an old-young runner, I reviewed the tables that grade performance with age. How did my 2:48.2 compare with the half-miles I ran years ago as a senior at Brooklyn Prep? A quick calculation showed that my mark in Eugene was equivalent to breaking two minutes—1:59.0 to be exact—something I could never do in high school.

And now in a way—in a great and glorious way—I had broken two minutes. Somewhere over Iowa, my eyes filled with tears.

E S S A Y

THE MESSENGER
BY MARC BLOOM

While George Sheehan was a prophet of the world, he was first and foremost a local runner from central New Jersey, hard by the Shore. I'd always see him at some small race with eighty-odd competitors on a windy day in Lakewood or Long Branch. He would breeze in from Omaha after lecturing to button-down doctors and racing a 10K, looking for the perfect antidote to a somber Sunday: another race.

Often George would compete in tights and bare chest, with his signature groans serenading those runners around him. In his waning years, when he slowed and could no longer hunt for a good time, race organizers set up the age groups to assure George would come away with an award.

The one Sheehan experience I'll treasure showed him racing in a different environment. It was a meeting I had with him one day in the late 1980s. I was writing an article on exercise and aging, and wanted to interview him. George was, of course, a great quote. Ask him what form of exercise is best, and George would say, "The one you'll do."

He told me to meet him at Freehold Raceway, a few minutes from my home, where his son John was a harness racing driver and trainer. We sat in the grandstand, and George gave me his spiel on how being fit adds life to your day, never mind days to your life. It was an ironic setting to be talking about health. All around us sad-looking people with bellies out to here were devouring junk food, smoking, and being consummate spectators.

And then it happened: Son John won his race, and George took off to congratulate him. We were seated in the upper deck. George weaved through the crowd, flew down the stairs, and ran out to the rail to embrace his son. I could barely keep up. George was then pushing seventy, and his energy and spirit astounded me. He was giddy with emotion.

Then it happened again: another victory, another post-race tear. It was warm and wonderful, and naturally I wrote it all down for my story.

In this episode George Sheehan, the messenger, had exemplified all that he preached. What could be more honest than that?

Marc Bloom, former editor of The Runner, *was George's editor when his columns appeared in that magazine. Currently, Bloom is a senior writer for* Runner's World, *track features writer for* The New York Times *and publisher of* The Harrier, *a cross-country newsletter.*

CHAPTER 12

TEAM SPORTS

One of the hundreds of parties spinning off from the Boston Marathon paid tribute to one of running's legends, a man with cancer. He was enduring heavy treatment that left him weak and cost him his hair, but he still managed to come to Boston. Marathoning's legends all try to get to Boston each April.

This wasn't George Sheehan's party. George, who hadn't looked healthier in years, was just one of the guests here to wish Fred Lebow well.

Lebow has a way of making things come out right. Even when his early prospects sound dim, the New York City impressario directs final acts worthy of Broadway.

I first met Lebow at the 1976 Boston Marathon. My first impression was that he talked oddly. It wasn't the way he talked, in an accent brought with him from Transylvania, but what he said. Fred spoke as a dreamer and schemer in a sport still conditioned to think small and to undersell itself. Running hadn't yet boomed. Jim Fixx said that same weekend of a book he was writing, "I hope it will sell ten thousand copies." It would sell a hundred times that many.

Lebow said of the marathon he directed, "We're taking it out of Central Park this fall and running it through all five boroughs. In a few years, this race could become bigger than Boston."

Dream on, I thought. Even if the city allows such a disruption, who would dare run on those mean streets?

Bill Rodgers dared, for one. He won the first four citywide races, and in those years New York City not only outgrew Boston, but all other marathons in the world.

Next Lebow noticed that as road racing picked up size and speed in this country, track interest waned. "If people won't go to track meets," he said, "we'll take the top track athletes to the people." He proposed a mile race along New York's Fifth Avenue. It won't work, I thought. Milers will feel as far out of their element here as Olympic swimmers would in the Central Park Reservoir.

The runners adapted. The Fifth Avenue Mile worked so well that it spawned a worldwide series of imitators.

Last year, Lebow said, "This country deserves a summer meet like those in Europe." He would direct the New York Games. I thought Fred was out of his element this time. He knew the road sport, but track was a different game that required selling tickets and not just giving away sidewalk space. His meet filled the stadium.

Fred Lebow's knack for directing successful finishes is now meeting its most serious test. Lebow isn't dealing with an event this time, but with his own life story. Co-workers suspected a problem this winter when Fred began talking oddly. His dreaming and scheming didn't alert them. That's how Fred normally talks. But it wasn't like him to slur words and forget names. He checked into a hospital to undergo tests.

The early and ominous suspicion was that he had a brain tumor. Doctors performed a biopsy in late February.

While Lebow awaited the results he told Dick Patrick of *USA Today*, "I'm prepared for anything. I've had a fulfilling life." The first diagnosis was inconclusive but still heartening. No signs of malignancy had been detected. Fred walked out of the hospital the same night he was diagnosed. A week later, he returned for treatment of a blood clot in his foot and a second biopsy.

These confirmed the worst fears: a cancer of the brain.

"It's not good," Lebow said. "But we know what it is that I'm fighting." The counterattack started immediately with a series of radiation treatments. "All I know is that if [the condition] is treatable and can be cured, I will be cured," he said. "I'm not being phony. I'm going to fight the hell out of it."

The fight will be uphill. But I've learned not to doubt Fred Lebow's ability to dream or scheme up a happy ending even when his odds sound longest.

He now turns first to George Sheehan for advice and support. George tells his friend to be patient, be strong. In many ways, says George, the worst of the disease comes first—the shocking news, the insults of early treatment, the coming to terms with fate. Things should get better.

§ § § § §

George Sheehan's marathons are finished. His races are shorter now, and they no longer promise any age-group prizes or personal records. George's racing has come full circle. He's back to the basics of his early days in the sport, when he ran purely for the sake of running.

So in Boston he sought out a generic race. "Across the Charles River," he wrote, "the Boston Marathon weekend was in full swing. A giant expo, lectures, clinics, panels, and hotel lobbies filled with celebrity runners." A world away at Fresh Pond in Cambridge, he found "a throwback to when running began. It goes back to when kids drew a line on the street, and the first one back was the winner. It is racing reduced to the essentials."

The field numbered only about one hundred. Lynn Jennings, the World Cross-Country champion, was here. George never saw her. The race director, old Fred Brown who has conducted these events since few know when, arrived ten minutes before the start. He carried a watch and a clipboard, the only tools needed for scoring this event. The event featured none of the pre-race ritual that, in George's words, "has assumed the solemnity of a High Mass." There was no signing up to do, no entry fee to pay, no bib number to pin on.

George asked the runner next to him for essential details. The man said, "You can run one lap, two-and-a-half miles, or two laps for the five-mile race. And you can make the choice as you go."

Fred Brown fired no starting gun. He just shouted, "Go!"

George wrote, "Within a few minutes, I realized that I was in with hardcore runners. My flat-out pace just about kept me in a group of a half-dozen bringing up the rear. One lap, I decided, would be enough." He had none of the usual amenities to help him along. No mile splits, no water stops, no encouraging onlookers. "Nor were there race officials keeping track of the runners. As a consequence, a friend and I missed a turn and thereby shortened the course by a quarter-mile of hills." Because generic races operate on the honor system, the two runners ran the missing loop in reverse so they would cover the full distance. At the end, they received sticks with place numbers on them. They gave these to a woman with the clipboard and had their names recorded. George watched some of the five-milers finish, then left. He had no reason to linger longer.

"There were no post-race refreshments, no awards ceremony. There was no need for them. We had done our best. We had wiped ourselves out. Now we were filled with the best refreshment or award a race can give—that wonderful langor that comes after strenuous effort."

§ § § § §

In common with most serious runners, George Sheehan was too proud to walk. Never mind that as his pace slowed, he ran slower than some people in races walked. He refused to join the walkers. Then he went to Thomasville, Georgia, to speak before a group gathering for a 5-kilometer walking event. "I tried not to be condescending about walking," he said of his talk. "Runners do not generally regard walking as a real sport, nor do they regard the walkers they pass on the road as real athletes. Until my visit to Thomasville, I shared that opinion."

To be a good guest, he entered the 5K walk, along with one thousand others. He recalled, "The starting line resembled some of the better-supported road races held every year—although most of the entrants did not have the lean, gaunt look I associate with runners. There were very few whippets in the field."

The 5K walk turned out to be both humbling and eye-opening. George thought his native endurance would see him through to a finish near the front, but he found his fastest possible walking pace to be "more demanding than expected. It was difficult to believe. I was at flank speed and doing exactly four miles per hour. Despite pumping my arms, using my hips and keeping my tempo as high as possible, I was barely able to keep up with the people around me. I would have been satisfied to stay with a group of middle-aged, somewhat overweight women just ahead. Try as I might, others who seemed to be out for a Sunday stroll crept farther and farther ahead."

An equal number of walkers finished in front of him and behind him. He viewed them all with new respect for the people he'd just joined.

"Walkers become fit and healthy athletes—and masters of their own sport," he wrote. "I met a thousand of them in Thomasville and became a believer."

§ § § § §

George Sheehan once labeled himself a "loner." It was hard to imagine, seeing him joining the crowds at races twice each weekend, or seeing him speak in packed auditoriums, or seeing him standing in the center of a crowd as he signed autographs and answered questions.

But that was the public Sheehan, and he spent only a small percentage of his time in public. By its nature, his writing was a solitary pursuit.

And when he raced, it was himself against the field. When he trained, it was by himself to do his thinking. Running, he said, was his "escape from people."

"There was a time when I rarely ran with anyone else," he wrote in a recent column. "I wanted to be alone with my thoughts when I was out on the road. Without a companion who might interrupt my stream of consciousness, I could follow any idea at any pace." George divided his sport into two parts: competition and contemplation, both essentially solo acts. Now he has added a third "C"—conversation, which must be a team sport.

He takes Saturday morning runs on the boardwalk with a group. He'd watched this group for years and wondered: Why would these people take a leisurely run when they could be going to a race? Why would they endure an hour of talk when they could be thinking? Now he knows the answers. "Where there were once too many people in my life, now there are too few. There was a time when I would have told anyone who asked to run with me that I had already run—when that was not true.

"Now I look forward to running with people. I need people to talk to. I need people to listen to. I need people to be with."

George went through a period when talks on the run were little more than extensions of his speeches. The other runners were his audience.

"Now I have real conversations. I have revived what had become a dying art in my life. I actually listen to what people have to say instead of simply waiting until they stop so I can talk. On the pleasant Saturday runs, there are no monologues. The ideas bounce from person to person. Topics surface and are gone. Paces vary. Places change. I run next to someone for a while, and then someone else takes his place."

After the run ends, the talk continues at a pancake restaurant. George wrote, "This is what the Dairy Queen was to my Little League sons, the part we will all remember best when we get older—who was there and what they said and what we ate."

Running is again his team sport. "While competition and solitude are both sources of happiness, there is yet another source of happiness to be found in running—a return to the companionship of youth and childhood.

"I now have comrades. I am a member of a gang."

E S S A Y

COLLECTING COLUMNS

BY CRISTINA NEGRON

I was terrified. That's how I felt when I sat in front of my computer, staring for the first time at George Sheehan's words filling the screen.

It was 1988. I had just been promoted from copy editor to associate editor at *Runner's World*. One of the jobs that came with the promotion was editing George's column. I knew that this man, more than forty years my senior, was considered the patron saint of runners. That he was a writer extraordinaire. So when I first faced his prose, I couldn't bring myself to change a word. If a sentence seemed too formal or too difficult to understand, I chalked it up to his "style" and didn't touch it.

Over the next several months, however, I learned that I could help make George's writing clearer without changing his style. When I begin editing his column, George requested that I send him a checking copy—a practice that I continued until his death. But he never called me with changes or complaints—only the occasional factual correction. "I got the name of that writer wrong," he'd say.

During the last year I worked with him, he did send back a column with a note scribbled on it. I thought, "Oh no, all these years without a problem, and now I've done something he didn't like."

I was wrong. He was finally paying me a compliment.

Well, sort of. On the top of the edited page, he wrote, "This is a really good column."

George's ego was one of his more endearing qualities. He wouldn't have been George without it.

So the first stage of my association with George was marked by intimidation. Once I got over that, I moved into stage two. I tried to be more than just a mechanics editor. I tried to guide him in certain directions, give him ideas, ask him for revisions. Stage two didn't last long.

George, I learned soon enough, did not take direction from anyone.

I'd heard him speak on many occasions, and I was always impressed. I'd scribble notes during his talks and later highlight those topics I felt would make wonderful columns for *Runner's World*. Then I'd send him a cheerful letter, praising him lavishly and suggesting he write on this thing or that thing from his speech.

He never told me "no." But he never did it, either. He wrote what he wanted, when he wanted, and that was it.

Sometimes he'd write a column that just hinted at running. Others had nothing at all to do with running. Some would be perfect if he'd just expand on one part or leave out another. I'd ask for revisions of that nature. Again, he simply did not do that. Once George finished an essay, it was done and he had no interest in ever working on it again.

This was pretty incredible to me. I knew, and every decent writer knows, that writing is rewriting.

Perhaps George had done all the rewriting he wanted to do before he sent his columns to me. Or maybe he was the Mozart of writers. Remember the scene in the movie *Amadeus* when Salieri discovers Mozart's original sheet music? It didn't have a single crossout, not a single revision. Mozart's genius went straight from his head onto the paper. I learned not to mess with Mozart.

By stage three, George and I settled into what would become our comfortable working pattern. He would send me ten or twelve manuscripts at a time, typewritten on long legal-size paper. I'd review them, keeping some for future use and sending back the others. I didn't give him any explanation for my rejects. I didn't ask him to revise. I simply gave him, per his request, a continuing record of what I had accepted, listed by first sentence. When it came time to edit a column, I'd pull it out, work on it, and send him the edited version. Then I wouldn't hear from him again (except on the occasions noted above).

When I think of George now, the thing that stands out the most is the way he drove himself to excel. He absolutely would not consider sitting back and resting. Even when I had enough of his work on hand to fill entire issues of *RW*, not just a single page, he was always worried that he needed to send me more. He'd call me and ask, "How are we doing with columns?"

In fact, only four months before his death he sent me this note:

> Dear Cristina:
> Should I panic yet? Working on a new column— selecting your best race—most people are running races that are too long.
> Do you have any good selections left? Please give me a deadline.
> Sincerely, George.

Cristina Negron, Runner's World *senior editor, fine-tuned George Sheehan's columns from 1988 to 1993.*

CHAPTER   1 3

COMING HOME

A rumpled businessman, ending his workday in New York City, shoved into the hotel elevator and studied his fellow riders. Everyone but him wore a tuxedo. He didn't notice, or didn't care if he did recognize him, that one of the passengers was the most decorated American Olympian of all time, Carl Lewis. "What is this," the businessman groused to no one in particular, "a convention of headwaiters?"

A better guess would have been Halloween partiers. The night was October 31, and these men in the elevator were dressed in most unusual costumes for them. You normally can't underdress among runners. "Dressing up" for a running party means wearing pants not made of denim, shoes other than nylon, and a shirt without a race name.

I'm a typical runner. I don't own a three-piece suit, and at age forty-eight I'd gone through two proms and two weddings without ever wearing a tux.

Until this night. The invitation to the *Runner's World* 25th-Anniversary gala read "black tie optional," but this manner of dress wasn't an option for staff. Only one exception was made—for George Sheehan.

Halloween night, most of the party guests went formal. The site was a theater a half-block off Broadway. This event was lavish but tasteful. It might have been a two-hour ad for the magazine but instead became a celebration of the sport's past quarter-century. It was a night for gawking at and talking with many of running's brightest stars. Never before had so many from such a wide time span gathered in one place.

Fifteen Olympic medalists attended, along with assorted world champions and recordholders. So deep was the guest list that many U.S. Olympians and Boston or New York Marathon winners didn't even reach the stage. The night featured an Oscars-style awards program. Broadcasters Marty Liquori and Tony Reavis emceed, and Bud Greenspan supplied custom-made films.

The awards were a vehicle for bringing the stars onstage so the crowd could see how they looked and sounded. Presenters spoke, too, and they made as illustrious a group as the receivers. The presenters included both Olympic women's marathon champions, Joan Samuelson and Rosa Mota, along with world recordholder Ingrid Kristiansen; Jim Ryun reuniting with Kip Keino, the man who beat him in the Mexico City 1500; American legends Mary Slaney, Alberto Salazar, and Bill Rodgers; three of the last four Olympic men's marathon winners, Frank Shorter, Carlos Lopes, and Gelindo Bordin. The winners included Billy Mills for the greatest Olympic upset—never mind that it occurred two years before *RW* was born—and Carl Lewis for top Olympic athlete. At this distance-centered event, the TV lights and cameras came on only for these sprinter-jumpers—Grete Waitz and Sebastian Coe, Athletes of the Quarter-Century. Waitz for leading women's marathoning into the modern era, Coe for twice winning the Olympic 1500 meters.

Most of these performers are still active as runners, some still at or near their best. The generations came together here to pay tribute to each other.

As the program ended, George Sheehan joined dozens of other guests onstage for a curtain call. He stood beside Johnny Kelley, who best represented the spirit of the evening. *Runner's World* publisher George Hirsch noted that Kelley had run his thirty-fifth Boston Marathon, at age fifty-eight, the year the magazine was born. This year, he ran his sixtieth Boston at eighty-three.

The parade of stars across the stage showed that running's leaders come and go with the seasons. Kelley showed that the running itself has a timeless quality.

§ § § § §

George Sheehan compromised on his costume for the Halloween-night party in celebration of the *Runner's World* birthday. He didn't wear a tuxedo, but did trade his usual jeans and sweater for a blazer and tie. This night wasn't meant to pat the magazine on its own back but to honor the sport at large. George played only a minor role in this production, but in this galaxy of stars he still shone as brightly as anyone.

He wasn't with *RW* when it started in 1966. He didn't arrive until four years later, and was absent from this magazine's pages for an extended period in the 1980s. But in the eyes of readers, he's the one person who gives the magazine its strongest voice and most human face.

Runner's World came to his old hometown to celebrate. Putting George, New York City, and the word "hometown" in the same sentence sounds odd to me. I know he was born and grew up in Brooklyn, went to college in Manhattan and to medical school on Long Island. But he never has seemed a New York kind of guy. He doesn't fit the upper-crust New York–professional stereotype, anyway. He looks and acts more like a small-town family doctor, ill at ease with city ways.

And yet this city remains his running home. Two careers started here, first as a high school boy in the 1930s and then as a reborn middle-aged athlete. In the 1960s, George began driving up from the Jersey Shore to race on the streets and in the parks of New York City. That almost-weekly habit continues even now, because this is where races are easiest to find and where the most of his old running pals gather. The largest of all Big Apple events is, of course, the New York City Marathon. It now draws about twenty-five thousand runners.

Runner's World scheduled its birthday party to coincide with the marathon this year. George has his own party here almost every year. An accident of scheduling causes this race to fall within a few days of George's birthday each year, and occasionally on the exact day, November

5. He turned sixty here in 1978, then seventy in 1988. He now looks forward to bringing his running gang together in his old hometown for a seventy-fifth-birthday party two years from now.

§ § § §

The day after this year's New York City Marathon, George Sheehan asked me, "Do you still have that collection of articles on the New York City Marathon we put together for *Time* magazine? I seem to have lost it." *Time* had printed George's series on the Boston Marathon, then asked for something similar on New York. He'd collected and submitted it, only to receive a polite no-thanks. He'd filed it away, as I had. He knew that my copy would be easier to retrieve than his.

Memories stirred by the latest New York City Marathon made him want to see if this work still had publication potential. It never saw print in the news magazine, but parts of it bear repeating here for the affection they show toward his old hometown and its most famous race.

George first told of this marathon's power to pull him into the city, even when he hadn't planned to be there:

> The Friday night before the New York Marathon, I spoke at a spaghetti dinner given by a local running club. Before the talk to one hundred runners and their families, I loaded up on the bread and beer and pasta. And I shared in the excitement and enthusiasm and anticipation they all felt.
>
> Then in the question-and-answer period that followed, someone asked me if I was going to run the marathon. Without hesitation, I answered, "Yes."
>
> Until that dinner, I would have said, "No." For the previous week, I had thought of any number of legitimate reasons not to run. Primarily I had not gotten in the necessary training.
>
> I had this all in mind when I rose to speak. I had even investigated the possibility of other races that day, a five-miler perhaps or some easy 10K. But the closest event I could find was in Richmond, Virginia. Then as I looked around at those runners, I knew I had to be in New York.

One of the worst feelings in the world is that of missing something—the feeling that everything is going on somewhere else.

That Friday night, I knew I wanted to join in the fight. It was easier to risk pain and embarrassment and failure and the possibility of walking home from the Bronx than to miss this great and wonderful struggle.

George's struggle took him to distances far beyond those he had covered in training. The effort was exhausting but not without humor, as he explained in this vignette:

> Near the twenty-three-mile mark of the New York Marathon, the course turns off Fifth Avenue into Central Park. The runners face a short but fairly steep and demanding hill, and then the course follows an undulating road through the park toward the finish.
>
> I entered the park in the grip of the inexpressible fatigue that comes at that stage in the race. I was once again engaged in the struggle between a completely exhausted body and a yet-undefeated will. I ran toward the hill, realizing that finishing was still problematical, fearing that I might still have to walk and knowing that no matter what happened, those final twenty-five or more minutes would constitute my most painful experience this side of major surgery. I ascended the hill past a small group of onlookers. One of them recognized me and called out, "Dr. Sheehan, what would Emerson have said now?"
>
> I had to laugh, even in that pain. It was a particularly deft shot at someone who had used other people's words to express his own truth—and I was now in a situation that clearly no one else could describe.

For George, the New York Marathon wasn't a sightseeing tour. He wrote:

> After I finished, my daughter asked me if I had relived my childhood while running thorough the streets of Brooklyn. Surely, she thought, those miles in Bay Ridge and along Fourth Avenue must have brought back memories of growing up in the city.
>
> Other spectators thought I must have been inspired by the breathtaking view at the start on Verrazano

Bridge, the helicopters hovering like fish in a giant mobile. And hadn't I been filled with emotion, they asked, as we passed from borough to borough, from bridge to bridge?

In truth, none of these things happened. My old Brooklyn neighborhood went unnoticed as I sought a speed somewhere between being rash and being prudent.

I was still adjusting my stride as I passed without a gaze the street where I picked up pizzas for my father. In those days, he must have been the only Irishman in Brooklyn who knew what a tomato pie was. And as I continued experimenting with my pace, I barely looked at the library on Pacific Street that I haunted while doing high school book reports.

The vista during a marathon is of no consequence. Degree of difficulty is what concerns me. Wind, sun, terrain, and weather are what I look to.

To me, a marathon is a marathon is a marathon. There is nothing else, just the matter of taking my body—five-feet-nine, 136 pounds, 9 percent body fat and 60 percent slow-twitch fibers—a distance of twenty-six miles, 385 yards. Everything that affects this accomplishment is important, everything else is irrelevant. I must focus not on scenery or on memories, but on the basics of marathon survival.

I will not deny, however, that every marathon is a memorable event. The finish of every one I have run will stay with me the rest of my life. The last mile through Central Park in New York is not something easily forgotten. There is nothing to compare to the feeling I get on completing a marathon. But I must not think of that until the end comes.

ESSAY

HE'S DAD

BY GEORGE'S DAUGHTERS

(Sung to the tune of "The Lady Is a Tramp")

He's called a guru from here to L.A.
They come by hundreds to hear what he'll say.
He says New Jersey's the place where he'll stay.
That's why the doctor is a champ.

He can't be bothered with political views.
Polite conversation will send him to snooze.
It's him and running, you don't get to choose.
That's why the doctor is a champ.

He likes the cool sea breeze in his hair,
what's left up there.
He's Dad, we're glad.

He drives his Honda like Ahab at sea.
Voids in a bottle when he has to pee.
Gets to the race but loses his key.
That's why the doctor is a champ.

Likes upper tummy with low body fat.
Skim milk and coffee will help him get flat.
High lipid profiles are not where it's at.
That's why the doctor is a champ.

He likes the cool sea breeze in his hair,
what's left up there.
He's Dad, we're glad.

He's ectomorphic in four shades of blue.
Grandpa's a name he'll always eschew.
He's Nanna's friend and Big George to you.
That's why the doctor is a champ.

He runs for cover when kids run amok.
He'll drink all evening and not spend a buck.
Won't turn you down when you're down on your luck.

That's why the doctor is a champ.

You walked the aisle with a living saint.
She's a real looker but stupid she ain't.
She stood beside you when they said she cain't.
That's why the couple are the champs.

He likes the cool sea breeze in his hair,
what's left up there.
He's Dad, we're glad.

She stood beside you when they said she cain't.
That's why the couple are the champs.

*George and Mary Jane Sheehan's daughters and daugh-
ters-in-law wrote and performed this song on George's
seventieth birthday, in 1988. They repeated it at his tribute
dinner five years later.*

CHAPTER 14

LAST RACE

Look past the boarded-up storefronts on Saginaw Street, the main drag of Flint. Forget Flint's "Roger and Me" image for now. (In fact, don't even breathe that documentary film's name to the city's boosters.)

To see the best of Flint, drop in on Crim Festival of Race weekend. Become part of what Lois Craig, the event's mother figure, likes to call "the Crim family." The event began fifteen years ago as local politician Bobby Crim's 10-mile race. Craig worked for him and inherited the race directing as one of her duties.

Her "family" now numbers close to twelve thousand. The day's events include the original 10-mile, plus an 8K and 5K runs, kids' races, and fitness walks. Once each year, the Crim family brings downtown Flint back to crowded and noisy, healthy and happy life. The runners and walkers fill Saginaw Street all of Saturday morning. They pack the hotels and restaurants all weekend. They give financially strapped Flint a jumpstart worth millions of dollars and contribute about $100,000 to the event's charity, the Special Olympics. Lois Craig conducts Crim in a family way. She bases invitations as much on personal loyalties as athletic abilities.

Craig brought George Sheehan into the family this year. He came here to speak, certainly, but also to schmooze with his honorary siblings. And, oh yes, to run if he wanted. If there's a race anywhere within reach, and if George is anywhere near fit, he wants to run it. He wouldn't hear of going for a shorter distance at Crim. It had to be the featured 10-mile race. This would be his longest one in quite awhile. But knowing that any race he ran now might be his last, he wanted to make it a major effort.

I was in Flint but missed seeing George run. TV-commentary duties occupied me during his race, then I hustled off to run one of the shorter distances while he was still out on the 10-mile course. Then we missed each other afterward. As is his custom when he travels to races, George rushed from the finish line to the airport to catch the first flight home. He figures that the race is the final act of his performance, and staying longer would be anticlimactic. Besides, he often has another race scheduled near home the next day.

I asked a Crim official if he'd seen George finish. "I did," said the official. "I don't know his time, but he was way back and looked bad coming in."

That's George, I told him. He always looks spent at the end of a race, especially when he runs his best.

§ § § § §

George Sheehan told me his Crim 10-mile race story by phone the following Monday morning. He and Jerry Loviska, who was injured, finished at the end of the line. Loviska bemoaned their slowness. George acknowledged that they took almost twice as long to finish as they once had. But he reminded his companion, "We're still doing the best we can with what we have." He didn't add, but might have, that no runner can do any more.

This would indeed be George's last race. I later urged him to write about it, but he never did. He had other more important topics in mind. He felt he'd written this story before. It was about competition, and he'd already given new meaning to that word—as well as to the term "friendly rivals."

An earlier essay of his told of competition at its best. He was running the last mile of a race when he heard someone coming up from behind. As the younger man pulled alongside and then ahead, George shouted, "Way to go. You're looking great."

George didn't surrender meekly but recalled chasing the man as best he could. "Until he challenged me, I had been running to survive, thinking I was doing the best I could. Now I discovered reserves I had not suspected were there. I finished with my best time of the year." He wrote that such encounters are "the rule rather than a rarity in running. They embody the essence of the running experience. Nevertheless, the younger man found my encouragement almost incomprehensible. The idea that an opponent would urge you to beat him seemed an impossibility. He became so psyched up, he said, that he ran better than he had thought possible."

This is competition at its best because you draw strength from other runners without draining any of theirs. You don't have to push anyone down to stand tall. George called this "the true nature of competition. The Latin root of the word is *petere*—to go out, to head for, to seek. The *com* is doing it together, in common, in unity, in harmony. "Competition, then, is simply each of us seeking our absolute best with the help of each other." Wish competitors well, said George, because "the better they do, the better I will do."

Competing with them makes you run harder, longer, faster than you could go alone. In this setting, George would find it "unthinkable to cheat anyone else or to be diminished by the performance of another." You feel no need to play physical or psychological tricks on your competitors.

This is the ideal way of viewing a race: runners all in it together, helping each other, working as a team to accomplish goals higher that each one might have reached alone, competitors becoming part of the same extended family.

§ § § § §

The healing is now complete in George Sheehan's immediate family. Out of respect for all the people involved, I'll mention few names and details, but will focus only on what George already has chosen to reveal about a now-closed chapter of his life.

His family fractured in the early 1980s when George moved away from home and in with another woman. They lived together for several years, and when they finally separated the pain was almost as intense as if a marriage had ended.

"When your life is going nowhere in particular," George has written of that episode, "there is nothing better than being knocked on your ass. Mindless mediocrity needs a hard right to the solar plexus. When you are in a permanent holding pattern, getting hit from the blind side may well be the best thing that can happen.

"When the woman I had lived with told me to leave, I felt as if all three events had happened simultaneously. I had no hint then that I would be able to pick myself up and make a fresh start, that eventually I would look back and see it as a necessary and good thing to happen. I was injured."

He felt alone and lost. He turned to friends for advice and found their words unsatisfying at first. "They made the event commonplace. Join the crowd, they said: It's tough for a while, very tough, but time heals.

"I heard the chorus: Hunker down, wait it out."

George came to realize that they were right. "Being knocked on my butt and punched in the stomach has been good for me," he said. "I have changed in ways I would not have believed possible or necessary, and explored areas of my mind never before penetrated."

One good friend had told him, "Look inside, George. There is a reason for this, but you alone will know it."

George added, "I know now that there *is* a reason, and see it clearly enough to make out the major features: the failure to live up to my own beliefs, the failure to develop them further, and the failure to see that my concentration on the mind and the body had atrophied my life with others."

His vision cleared. It eventually pointed him toward home and the embrace of the family that had waited out his wanderings.

§ § § §

Strangers feel they know George Sheehan from the highly personal way he writes and speaks. They often approach him, introduce themselves, and lead him into conversation. As he finished a recent swimming workout at the Shore, a runner acted out this familiar scenario. Their brief talk led the stranger to ask, "What is the most important thing in your life?"

George was tempted to launch into a lengthy philosophical discourse on the meanings of importance and of life. But stripped almost bare, as he was for swimming, he reduced his thoughts to the basics as well. "My answer was simple and direct as the newly risen day," he wrote. "Without hesitation, my head and heart responded that the most important thing in my life is my family."

Quick as the word "family" jumped to mind this day, George had been slow to arrive at this answer. "When our children were born," he said, "I was primarily concerned with my self-development. My wife and family were part of that self only peripherally.

"They were in intimate association with me. I was responsible for their growth and development. But they were nevertheless external to the self I was making."

While pursuing his second career as a running celebrity, George became even more preoccupied. He admitted that "at times I wanted to be free from the hassle of family life. My solution was to more or less detach myself from the group. In that position, I was not a positive influence, but at least I wasn't a negative force." He wasn't truly reclusive. He liked having people around, "but I preferred to read a book while they were there."

Adversity, which he calls "a lifegiving force," turned him homeward. "Cancer and its attendant pain, and an awareness of my isolation, brought me back to a patient, loving wife and our sons and daughters. In giving me cancer, fortune had smiled on me. Pain was a key to opening up a new and larger life. That's why I was able to answer without hesitation when a stranger asked me to put my present life in one word. Family."

§ § § § §

One duty to family, both immediate and extended, that George Sheehan thinks he has neglected is giving thanks. One of the finest columns he ever wrote came out at Thanksgiving time:

> This is the day on which we thank the Lord for His blessings. It should also be a day when we stop, then think, then thank our fellow human beings.
>
> Yet I rarely do. People are nice to me, and I think nothing of it. I've failed to express gratitude to any number of individuals who have contributed to my life. Thank-yous are so easy to say yet so rarely uttered. So few of us speak the words directly, or write a note, or pick up the phone to express our appreciation. Many times, we think "thank-you" but never say it. More often, however, it is simply a matter of not thinking.
>
> It is true that our happiness should not depend on what other people think about us. Nevertheless, it can undoubtedly be enhanced by good wishes and good words that go from heart to heart. We thank the Lord for His blessings. We should also stop, then think, then thank our fellow human beings.
>
> There are people who had a major influence on our lives and never knew it. There are people we loved and left who could be told that those loving years were a gift we still treasure. There are lives that have intertwined with our own in helpful and meaningful ways. For all these people, it's never too late to give thanks.

E S S A Y

DEAR GEORGE
BY PRESIDENT BILL CLINTON

I am pleased to add a voice in praise of George Sheehan from the middle of the pack. Through your books and more than two decades of columns in *Runner's World*, you have been an inspiration to many of us.

As the guru and philosopher king of running, you have informed and motivated us to follow your teachings. We have learned that we are all heroes in our own right. You have shown us that we run best when we run with the simple joy of children, and that running and racing give us the chance to become in fact what we already are in design.

You have expanded the boundaries of our knowledge about sports medicine, about the relationships between exercise and health, and about ways we can all lead optimally effective and energetic lives. You have shown us how to achieve personal bests, not just in our individual quests, but also in other areas—at work, with our families, within our communities.

As your pace has slowed and you have come back to us in the pack, you have felt the loving concern from hundreds of thousands of us. Your courageous disclosures of prostate cancer have brought forth great warmth and continuing respect from runners everywhere.

· George, you may be getting slower, but you have never displayed more grace and courage. You're an inspiration to us all, and you should know we are with you in your valiant fight.

Newly inaugurated President Clinton, a regular runner himself, wrote this letter to George Sheehan in April 1993. It was read at George's tribute dinner.

George Sheehan in the late 1960s, as his work as a running writer is beginning for
local newspaper in New Jersey

George Sheehan (middle) is an outstanding miler for Manhattan College. He runs 4:19 in 1939.

Dr. George Sheehan (top row, fifth from right) and his Navy physician-training class prepare to ship out to the South Pacific in 1944.

The house in Rumson, New Jersey, where George and Mary Jane raised their 12 children

George circles the well-worn path of his home course in 1968.

George completes the 1989 New Jersey waterfront five-mile race in his home area.

In 1965, rejuvenated runner George chases his youngest son, Michael, around the track laid out in their backyard.

George finishes a mid-1980s Falmouth (Massachusetts) Road Race with his friend George Hirsch.

George joins Bill Rodgers, then America's finest marathoner, at a 1980 dinner where they share the stage.

Two Georges, Hirsch (future publisher of *Runner's World*) and Sheehan, recover and celebrate after a Boston Marathon in the mid 1970s.

One of George's proudest moments as an athlete – running the World Veterans Games 800 meters as a 70-year-old. He's in the lane nearest the camera.

George Sheehan and Jim Fixx, running's two best-selling authors, take their message to the streets.

One of the dozens of races George ran in New York City's Central Park. This event is the 1983 Trevira Twosome.

George travels to his ancestral home, Ireland, in the mid-1980s. He runs here with J.P. Murray, a writer for *Irish Runner* magazine.

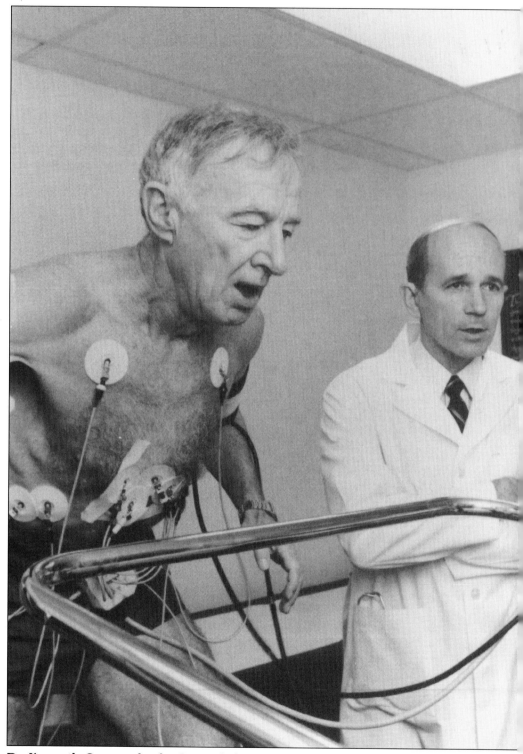

Dr. Kenneth Cooper checks George's fitness on a treadmill at the Aerobics Center in Dallas in the late 1980s.

George finishes the 1982 Marine Corps Marathon, which passes the historic sites of Washington, D.C.

George sets the world mile record for men 50 and older, running 4:47.7 in this 1969 race at Cornell University.

George visits his longtime editor Joe Henderson in Eugene, Oregon, during the 1989 World Veterans Games.

George joins an autograph session with fellow author Jim Fixx, shortly before Fixx's sudden death in 1984.

Joining George at the Washington Monument are (left to right) Senator Richard Lugar, Marty Cooksey, and Frank Shorter.

Mary Jane and George during a 1990 trip to Sydney, Australia

Mary Jane, George's wife of 49 years, gives her interpretation of the Sheehan story.

George speaks to 500 friends and family at the April 1993 dinner.

George, eldest in a family of 14 children, with his sister Mary, who spoke at his dinner.

Two of running's legends, George Sheehan and Johnny Kelley, meet at the *Runner's World* 25th birthday party in New York City, 1991.

George's swim at Rehoboth Beach, Delaware, in September 1993 with sons (left to right) Tim, Andrew and John

The Sheehan family vacations at Rehoboth Beach: (left to right) Nora, John, Andrew, George and Mary Jane.

George warms up after his Rehoboth Beach swim with granddaughter Abigail Adams at his side.

At home in Ocean Grove in his room facing the Atlantic shore in late October 1993

George Sheehan, 1918 – 1993

PART III

GOODBYE & THANKS

(1993)

GEORGE SHEEHAN TIMELINE FOR 1993:

April	Honored at dinner attended by 500 at Atlantic Highlands, New Jersey
April	Gives last speeches at Boston Marathon and Manchester, Vermont
July	Travels to Emmaus, Pennsylvania, for final interview to appear in *Runner's World*
September	Joins family for a vacation at Rehobath Beach, Delaware
October	Completes material for his final book, *Going the Distance*
November 1	Dies at home in Ocean Grove, New Jersey, with his family at his side. Survived by his wife, seven sons, five daughters, 17 grandchildren, four brothers, five sisters

C H A P T E R   1 5
LAST SUPPER

George Sheehan is dying. No one but George himself wants to use the word, of course, but everyone who knows him knows that he won't live much longer.

That's why so many people sat down to dinner with him here this weekend. That's why I flew across the country to be here.

George fought his disease to a standstill for most of the past seven years. His cancer didn't advance significantly, but neither did it retreat miraculously. The illness was always there at the borders of George's defenses, waiting for an opening that it knew would appear someday. Its time came last fall. George called me in October 1992 with the news. He always has shared his news soon after receiving it himself.

"I'm in bad shape this time," he said then. "I can't run, I can barely walk, and I have a hard time even standing on stage long enough to give a talk."

He told of going into a new round of radiation treatments, of trying new drug therapies, of canceling trips to make medical care his full-time job. He said, "My doctor told me if I don't do this, I may not last another two months."

That was six months ago. George had proved doctors' predictions wrong before, and he has stared down death again. He took some of the treatments but later rejected some of the more radical experiments. He couldn't run and probably never will again, but he went back to walking.

He also returned to speaking. He never stopped writing.

In fact, now that he's facing the final deadline he probably writes more than ever before. And maybe better. Certainly more personally. George never has sought any sympathy for his condition. But neither has he held any secrets.

His stories appear first in a local newspaper. As word went out there that his final battle had been joined, some local friends decided, "We've got to do something to honor him. We can't wait until after he's gone, either. We have to do it soon."

Tim McLoone took charge of the planning. He's an ex-running star and race director who plays in bands and owns a restaurant-bar in George's home area. Tim first suggested a surprise party. George Sheehan III, who works with his dad, nixed that idea right away.

"We'll never be able to keep a secret in this family," said son George.

Young George then broached the subject with his dad. Dr. George's first reaction: "Definitely not! An event like this would be too hard for me to handle."

"Fine," said the son. "It's your call."

"The next morning," young George recalled later, "he came into the office with ten pages of notes. They told where the party could be held, what the program might include, and who should be invited."

Later, the Doc (as he's known locally) started to worry that no one would come. "I gave a recent talk in Florida, and only ten people showed up," he said. "What if that happens here?"

"No chance of that," the son reminded the dad. "We'll draw a crowd with the Sheehans alone."

Just to be safe, Dr. George extended the invitation list. He then gave his okay to publish an announcement in local newspapers. About that time, *Runner's World* came into the act. Publisher George Hirsch signed on as a speaker, and editor Amby Burfoot called me to make sure I'd be there. I wouldn't have missed it.

By the time I left home, the guest list stood at three hundred and was still growing. Young George said, "We could top four hundred." It would grow to five hundred.

§ § § §

Dr. George had called me to say, "You're staying with us, aren't you?" He meant at the Sheehans' hotel, overlooking the Atlantic at Ocean Grove. They no longer rent rooms but still fill them regularly with sons and daughters, cousins, in-laws, and grandchildren. I'd visited there briefly two other times but had never stayed in Chez Sheehan.

Nor had I gotten to know any of the family besides George, Mary Jane, and George III. I'd meet Sheehans by the dozens this weekend.

Fittingly, I would see the number-one Sheehan first. He'd told me, "I'll be coming back from Texas that morning, and we could meet at the airport. My son George will be picking me up there."

He'd given four talks in Tyler, Texas, that Friday. Then stood out in the cold for three hours to watch the race on Saturday before driving to Dallas for a party in his honor. Then taken the first flight to Newark Sunday morning. I'd flown in the night before and stayed in an airport motel. Now I waited alone at the American Airlines gate for George to come off his plane.

This was my first glimpse of him since Halloween 1991, at the *Runner's World* 25th-Anniversary party. We'd talked at least once a week since then, and as usual George had hidden nothing about his condition. But hearing about it wasn't the same as seeing its effects. I stood back against the wall and watched for him to come out the jetway.

A wheelchair waited at the gate. I wondered briefly if it was for George, but then saw him walking out—wearing his trademark uniform of blue jeans, blue shirt, and blue sweater. From a distance he looked much like before. He didn't appear any thinner. Before he spotted me, though, I could see how much he'd slowed. The cancer had spread through his bones, mainly in the lower back and upper legs. Now it had taken the athlete's bounce from his step. He walked in a stiff, pained shuffle.

He saw me as I came close enough for a good look.

The color had gone out of him since our last meeting. His hair was whiter, but the big change was in his face. The once-rosy Irish cheeks were now pale.

After our greetings, George made two telling comments. The first was a question. "Can you take my bag?" he asked. It was a light carry-on but still too much for his sore back.

Then he said, "I woke up yesterday feeling like I'd played a quarter in the NFL. I hurt all over."

He'd said to himself at the time, "This is it. I'm canceling my future talks. I'm finished."

He already was renegotiating his terms of surrender. But he knew that the strain of traveling and speaking would soon become too heavy to bear.

§ § § § §

George Sheehan took me home to meet the reuniting family. One of my aims on this trip was to meet as many of the "kids" (who range from the early thirties to late forties) as possible. The family's party had started early, without George, and it would run late. It had begun on Saturday with a celebration of Sarah's fortieth birthday.

The crowd early Sunday afternoon was still fairly small, though about a dozen Sheehans and their relatives had already gathered. Their number would grow by a factor of five. Mary Jane gave George his final instructions before we left for the main event: "Make sure there are sixty tickets for us and we're all sitting together."

After an exchange of greetings, my next item of afternoon business was a run along George's beloved boardwalk. Or what used to be that wooden walkway. A big storm blew in from the northeast last December. The waves ate away most of the beach and stacked the walk's boards like tinkertoys. It looked as if some higher power knew that George Sheehan didn't need his favorite running surface anymore. Or maybe the damage was a visible reminder to him of what he could no longer do.

I took a run along George's old route with his son Andrew, the family's other writer. After college, he'd signed on with the newspaper where his dad's column appeared. Andrew's rise in this business then took him to Pittsburgh and into a lengthy strike shutdown of his paper. A Pittsburgh TV station lured him out of print journalism and in front of the camera. He's just back from reporting on Croatia for the quarter-million Croats who settled in the Pittsburgh area. While there he shot ten segments for the local news.

"We were so busy there that I didn't have much time to think about what was happening," he said. "Only after I got home did the devastation and hopelessness of that war hit me. One day, I couldn't stop crying."

George said as we drove to the dinner that night, "Andrew isn't like the rest of us. He talks about his feelings and asks about ours. The rest of us try to avoid doing that."

Thus prompted, I asked George, "So how are you feeling on the brink of this event?"

"Terrified," he answered without hesitation. Terrified, I knew, at having to bare his feelings to so many people who are so close to them—and at having so many of them open up to him in return.

§ § § § §

The event frightened George but attracted him, too. Doors at the Shore Casino didn't officially open until five o'clock, but he couldn't wait that long. We got there almost an hour early. Tim McLoone, the master of ceremonies, and George Hirsch of *Runner's World*, a key speaker, tried to shoo Dr. George away as he walked in on their rehearsal.

"He won't even notice," I told them. "He'll soon be too busy talking."

And so he was. The crowd—*his* crowd—couldn't wait to get there, either. Long before five, the room was well on its way to filled. I knew few of these people. This both surprised and pleased me, because it showed George to be much more than a running specialist. He has traveled in many circles: family, running and writing circles, medical, school, and community circles. These circles all joined here for perhaps the first time.

We talked, we drank (well, *they* drank; I never reached the overcrowded bar for my usual nonadult beverage), we ate. This all took three hours but was only the warmup for the marathon to follow.

Paying tribute to George Sheehan takes a long time. He has lived almost seventy-five very full years, and the program planners couldn't leave out any of his phases. The program took almost three hours to cover them all. Tim McLoone, a Billy Crystal-like performer, tried with little success to hurry the show along so we could hear from George himself before midnight. The show took roughly a chronological course. Double-Sister Mary, who's both George's sibling and a Catholic nun, led off. She told of their growing up in Brooklyn amid a family of sixteen. Then followed boys-turned-old-men from George's high school, college, and Navy days. We skipped ahead to his running revival and his second career in writing. George's oldest son and his wife spoke for the family. All the female Sheehans except Mary Jane sang him a parody song called "That's Why the Doctor Is a Champ."

Finally, on the far side of ten o'clock, George himself came to the stage. He betrayed little of the slowness that I'd seen in his step earlier that day. Before he took his turn on stage, the bar had become more crowded and noisy with each passing speaker. Now the room fell totally silent as the guest of honor began his talk. His voice came out quiet, slow, and a little hoarse at first. But as he warmed to his topic and the audience, this became the George Sheehan we'd always known: lively, eloquent, funny, and heartfelt. Everyone else had taken care to avoid the subject that brought us all here. No one dared call this a farewell party, though we all knew it was. He himself referred to the tribute meal as "the last supper."

George didn't hesitate to mention what everyone knew he faced. He said, "Dying is my current experience. I'm going to look at it and find out what it's all about."

The night ended with an emotional showing of family slides, set to music on videotape. Then the guests took another hour saying their goodbyes to George, who along with the other Sheehans was last to leave the casino. We'd spent seven hours there.

§ § § § §

Another two hours passed at Chez Sheehan before the place quieted down. I never did hear the last of the sons arrive back from their rounds. I was to leave at seven o'clock the next morning. Mary Jane was up as expected, and— efficient mom that she still must be—offering me tea and toast. Young George was up. He wore the same clothes as the night before and looked like he hadn't been home for long.

Dr. George was awake, too. This surprised me until he said, "I didn't sleep at all." Mornings-after are like this for him now. He can still psych himself up for a big performance, still go out and speak, still thrill the audience and be stirred by it. But this work costs him. The adrenaline rush makes him forget his new limits, and he stands and talks too long. This happened in Texas earlier in the weekend. He'd overextended himself on Friday and could barely get out of bed the next day. He never wanted to speak again. Yet he couldn't tell five hundred family members, friends, and fans that he didn't want to see them on Sunday. So again he pushed too far.

After the adrenaline retreated, the pain wouldn't let him sleep. Now he stood in the kitchen at dawn, looking more pale and stooped and frail than I'd ever seen him. He wore red sweatpants and a long-sleeved, white T-shirt. We said our goodbyes with a quick hug. My parting comment was, "We'll talk soon." We both knew this might be the last time I'd see him.

Everyone had known the same the night before. Few of us will see George again.

Young George said as we were leaving town, "We're a lucky family. Both parents have lived into their seventies, and all twelve of their children and the children's children are still here and healthy. Think how great the odds are that something serious would have happened to one or more of us."

Dr. George's condition is now serious. But he's also going on seventy-five and has been married for almost fifty of those years. Few of us will ever look back on a more productive lifespan. Even with his finish line in sight he feels fortunate. He had an early wake of sorts, when he could be there to enjoy it with five hundred of his nearest and dearest people. We should all be so lucky.

E S S A Y

RUNNING MATES
BY MARGARET MASON

I never got to run with him.

George Sheehan and I had talked about his more leisurely runs of recent years, and someday I was going to show up on his Ocean Grove, New Jersey, porch, trot along the ocean for a few miles with him and his friends, and then we'd all go out for breakfast.

I could feel the air and hear the gulls, and conjure up the repartee. But most of all I could imagine the joy, the unabashed celebration of being that a run down the road can bring out in some of us. This revel in running shoes has connected us once again with each other, with ourselves, and with the universe.

More than anyone in this world George Sheehan seized and articulated ephemera like that, and maybe I wanted to see for myself that our leader ran as he wrote. To share a moment with the man who so compellingly called us out to play; no matter the gray head, the white beard, or the spidery legs, we could become as children. We could become ourselves.

Running can invite some strange thoughts, and George Sheehan encouraged us to articulate mysterious, amazing, and inexplicable experiences.

"The road becomes a laboratory," wrote Sheehan, "where we subject what we have been taught to the test of this viable experienced universe... Somehow in the relaxation, the letting go, we arrive at a state which Heraclius described as 'listening to the essence of things.' We open ourselves to the world.

"And what of the soul? This hour allows, as does no place else, the freedom of seeing yourself as you are. Where better to examine your life, or your conscience, or to say your prayers?"

Crouched between the library stacks one afternoon, I devoured those words and others that Sheehan penned straight off the road, straight from his heart. I was delighted to know that it wasn't some starry-eyed twenty-year-old so elegantly describing my runner's high, my rush of authenticity, but a respected cardiologist, then in his fifties. Simultaneously, I realized how bizarre all of this was. I, a woman of a certain age who had never run before, seemed to have stumbled on an essential answer to life—at least my life—and I found a total stranger, Sheehan, talking about the same thing.

Running, he admitted, was an odd way to find the meaning of life, and he then proceeded to write page after page of insights—the kind that make you stop breathing for a second—gleaned on the road and from such friends as Emerson, Thoreau, William James, Marianne Moore.

George Sheehan seemed to have a special affection for women runners of all ages. "When I see women running," he wrote fifteen years ago, "I see a new world coming."

And somewhere else: "The woman who comes to know herself to be truly a runner has discovered not only her body, but her soul as well."

You can imagine my delight when I first met Sheehan a few years ago on the speakers' circuit. I was an unlikely groupie—I of a half a century and the ten-minute mile— and I was intimidated by this doctor, author, *Runner's World* columnist, speaker and possessor (in his fifties!) of a 4:47 mile. But there he stood in his pale blue denim shirt, jeans, and running shoes, and looked me straight in the eye. "Are you," he asked, "a runner?"

The angels sang. I *have* become an athlete, a word I never would have applied to myself if I had not read

George Sheehan. He always said, "Do the best you can with what you have." That stays with me, as do dozens of other lines.

The last time I saw George Sheehan, he seemed almost translucent. There was an ongoing quality about him, as if he were between two worlds. We all knew he was dying of prostate cancer. But in some ineffable way it didn't seem to matter. It seemed like a detail, part of who he was. Sheehan always talked openly about his cancer, for here was a man who often told his children, "There are no bad experiences."

That's another line that will go with me forever. What could I mean, that I didn't get to run with him? I—and thousands of others—run with him every day.

Margaret Mason lives in Appleton, Wisconsin. Her essay originally appeared in The Washington Post.

CHAPTER 16

LAST SPEECHES

George Sheehan wouldn't miss a Boston Marathon. He ran his first marathon here in 1964, and twenty more in a row after that.

He wrote during those years that since 1964 "running has been the hub of my life. From my running has radiated virtually everything I do and am. It has restored my body, given back my unspent youth, uncovered my creativity, become a source of my self-expression. Running has given me a self-esteem, an independence, a trust in my own experience. I have had a rebirth.

"But running, like any hub, needs an axle," he added. "It must have a center around which to revolve, a focus that gives stability and direction and purpose. My axle is the Boston Marathon."

Even after George stopped running at Boston, he kept returning here as an honored speaker at this unofficial national convention of runners. Boston's history and date give the event its convention status. Runners have been coming here for almost one hundred years, and for most of that time this was America's only truly national marathon. The race traditionally runs on a Monday, and this gives runners the weekend to convene before they compete. They come to Boston to celebrate the return of spring.

George once asked in a column, "What makes the Boston Marathon great? Is it, perhaps, April?

"The Boston Marathon preempted April, leaving other and lesser months to other and lesser marathons. It has taken the April of Chaucer's gentle showers, when people 'long to go on pilgrimages.' It has seized the April of T.S.

Eliot: 'The cruelest month breeding/Lilacs out of dead land mixing/Memory and desire.'

"The poets tell it all. Scatter-brained April, so unpredictable but still our best hope. Behind lies the long, hard, and possibly futile winter; ahead a perfect day and a perfect marathon?"

Note that he ended with a question mark. He always came to Boston in search of the perfect race but usually left with less. One of his most memorable essays dealt with imperfection. He wrote about the final miles of a marathon that seemed endless:

"Finally I was in Boston now and should have been home free. I wasn't. I was running a poor marathon, and when you run a poor marathon you not only hurt, you hurt longer. I had been out on the roads longer than any time in my fourteen years of running. But through all the pain and not knowing whether I would finish, and dragging out those last terrible miles, I always felt safe. I knew I was surrounded by friends and family and those who would take care of me no matter what.

"And knowing, too, that if I stopped they would say, 'You gave it your best, George.' Knowing whatever I did, I would not disappoint them. There would always be a meal and a soft bed and a good day for running tomorrow. Only the child still lives in a world where such days are possible."

§ § § § §

George Sheehan can't run marathons anymore, but he still comes to Boston in April, in search of days like this. The disease has taken his running legs, but he can still stand before these runners and speak of the experiences they all share. He can come to Boston and be surrounded by friends and family who'll take care of him no matter what. They know he'll give them his best. He'll know he won't disappoint them.

At Boston he speaks to his most sophisticated crowds— and some of the largest. They not only are marathoners, but those who had to meet time standards to run here.

These are the marathoners who train harder and know more than those who didn't qualify. They all read George Sheehan. Many of them have heard him speak before, possibly in this same room.

But George's fans keep coming back, the way a movie fan might watch *Casablanca* or *Gone with the Wind* repeatedly. Like the timeless films, Sheehan speeches are classics. His themes are well known, yet he never gives exactly the same talk twice. He speaks without notes and adds new twists each time. Listeners come to hear the familiar and to be surprised.

George was scheduled to talk on Sunday, the day before the marathon, at a *Runner's World* clinic in a Boston hotel. He drove up from New Jersey with Mary Jane on Saturday, steeling himself for the six-hour trip with extra painkillers. The Sheehans attended a party thrown by one of the shoe companies that night. The strain of traveling and socializing, along with effects of the medication, left George so weak and ill that he collapsed on the way back to his hotel.

"His talk at the runners' clinic was the following day," said Mary Jane. "He delivered it in fine style. I was surprised that he did so well, considering his condition the night before."

But as soon as George finished speaking and walked down the aisle, his wife instantly recognized the toll that the weekend had taken. A doctor friend had to step forward and help him back to his room. Rather than stay any longer amid the swirl of Boston activity and its attendant obligations, the Sheehans decided to drive home that night.

Mary Jane suggested that George see his doctor on Monday for a checkup. He declined, saying, "I'm feeling better already."

§ § § § §

George had more travel plans that same week, again going by car to New England, this time with his son

George III driving. They attended a runners weekend that Bill Rodgers hosted in Manchester, Vermont.

The weekend had a strong Boston Marathon flavor. Rodgers is a four-time winner of that race. Two of his co-stars were Joan Benoit Samuelson and Tom Fleming. Samuelson, the first women's Olympic Marathon gold medalist, had won two Bostons—once in world-record time. Fleming, who lives near the Sheehans in New Jersey, had twice placed second at Boston.

"We got there in time for a welcoming party on Friday night," said son George. "About fifty or sixty people were there, and Bill asked Dad to say a few words. He gave a half-hour talk, and at the end of it I could sense that he was in pain. He felt too bad even to go to dinner after that. He just wanted to have some soda, rest on a heating pad and take more painkillers.

"The next day he wasn't really any better. He sat on a panel with Billy, Joanie, Tom, and several other speakers, and wasn't focusing on what they were saying. He looked like he was really on a fade."

When that program ended, he told his son, "We'd better go home." George felt too weak to walk the long corridor back to their room at the Equinox Hotel, so he sat upfront with Joan Samuelson while young George packed and then drove the car around for the trip home.

This would be his last working trip. His only other travel would be to family gatherings.

George thought at the time that he'd failed—failed his hosts and failed himself as a speaker. He later told me by phone, "It reminded me of how I felt the time I dropped out at Boston."

I reread the column he'd written at the time:

"I could hear the crowd encouraging me. Some called out, 'Looking good.' Others yelled, 'You can make it.' The more perceptive shouted, 'Tough it out,' and, 'Hang in there.'"

"Now I was reduced to my private little hell, my eyes fixed on my shadow in front of me, watching this pantomime... I was virtually running in place.

"Then I felt a hand and looked up. There was a friend

beside me. She was watching the race and, seeing me in this state, she had rushed out."

"Don't you want to walk, George?" she asked. He described her as sounding like a mother talking to a child. George kept trying to run, and she repeated the question. Looking into her face "full of sympathy and care and love," he knew then that his race was over.

He told the friend, "Nina, all I want is someone to take me home." She put him on a trolley to the finish line that day in Boston. This day in Vermont, son George drove his dad home.

§ § § §

After the Vermont episode George did visit his doctors. They discovered that his blood count was alarmingly low. In effect his body was operating as if it were at an extremely high altitude because it was starved for oxygen. "I'm living at thirty thousand feet," he said.

At about the same time word of his condition spread along the runners' network from New England to a medical friend of George's in Palo Alto, California. Dr. Walter Bortz is an expert in aging actively. Dr. Bortz called George and asked bluntly, as perhaps only one doctor could say to another, "Do you want to live any longer?" He was testing to see if George had surrendered yet.

"Sure, I want more time," George said. "But my prospects don't look too good right now. I'm wearing out."

Dr. Bortz told him, "I'm treating several patients with conditions just like yours, elderly men with advanced prostate cancer. All of them are being helped tremendously by monitoring their blood counts and taking transfusions."

Bortz predicted this regimen could give George six more months. And he said they would probably be good months, certainly far better than he could expect without the treatments. George agreed to check with his local doctors. They concurred, and he received a transfusion immediately.

I talked to him by phone right before and soon after this first treatment. Before, he'd sounded like a 45 RPM record playing at 33. After, he was back up to normal speed.

Son George witnessed this transformation. "Dad took the blood and was rejuvenated," he said. "He showed more energy and vitality that we had seen in a long time."

George began responding to wellwishers by saying, "I'm supposed to be dying, but I don't feel like it. This could be embarrassing. I may hang around too long."

He wants to be around long enough so no work will be left undone. He wants to finish one more book, and now looks forward to spending at least the spring and summer with it. He calls it his "Death Book." Knowing that no publisher would accept that stark a title, I suggest—so far without success—that he call it "Miles to Go." That line comes from Robert Frost's poem: "I have promises to keep/and miles to go before I sleep." It best describes how George has lived with his illness since 1986. In fact, he used Frost's words himself when first revealing the cancer. George has gone many miles, and intends to travel more.

He has kept his promises. He has demonstrated what he calls "a healthy way to be ill." He has lived by his own line that there is nothing more certain than the victory of a man who will not give up. He has run all those races, written all those columns, published all those books, given all those talks. More importantly, he has ended a long separation from his wife and eased the resulting strains with their twelve children. By his own admission he has become less self-absorbed, and quicker to say his thank-you's and I-love-you's.

George's illness has taken him off the roads and off the stage. But his mind remains sharp and his will is still strong. His doctors have given him the time and energy, and his friends and family the support, to push toward one more big finish line way off in the distance.

E S S A Y

VICTORY LAPS
BY HAL HIGDON

The rules of life include birth and death. If you can't accept the latter, you shouldn't show up for the former.

George Sheehan knew that. He predicted cancer would claim him long before it was diagnosed. In 1978 we had breakfast together in Chicago before one of his lectures. George ordered scambled eggs and bacon, seemingly a high-cholesterol diet for a practicing cardiologist.

"Our family doesn't die of heart attacks," he joked. "We die of cancer. You need to understand your heritage. If you know what's going to kill you, you can eat accordingly."

Later, Dr. Sheehan modified his diet somewhat. But that was mainly because his writing for magazines and in eight books had made him a role model for many runners.

George was far from that when I first met him on the starting line of the Boston Marathon in the mid-1960s. Back in that era runners were so few in number that any newcomer was instantly spotted by the Old Hands.

George was among several doctors who began running Boston at that time. This served to legitimize running, proving not merely that the sport might be safe but that it could offer an outlet for those possessing ordinary talent but with extraordinary goals. Boston was no longer the province of the crazies, but could be considered the ultimate sanity.

The running boom would not begin for another decade. By that time George Sheehan was an Old Hand, ready to offer newcomers his philosophy that though running seemed hard, it could be "a purifying discipline that uses the body with passion and intensity and absorption." Although various people have been credited with igniting the running boom, George certainly provided one of the sparks, then fanned it. During a lecture at the 1993 New York City Marathon I reminisced about my old friend.

This prompted someone in the audience to ask, "What words of Dr. Sheehan do you remember most?"

George was a philosopher who avidly read the works of other philosophers. He was fond of quoting them, and now I found myself quoting him from his book, *This Running Life*. George regarded running as a form of play. In that book he wrote, "Play is our first act. If we are lucky, it will be our last. Once you've found your play, all else will be given to you."

Not only did George accept running as play, but he refused to take seriously his own position as the sport's reigning philosopher. The Boston Marathon finishes on Boylston Street. Marathoners coming down that final stretch find themselves cheered by thousands of spectators. George often told of a friend who informed him, "Doc, one block of Boylston Street you're just another skinny Irishman."

But runners knew him as more than that. I still have this picture in my mind of George running those final yards on Boylston, pulling off the knotted handkerchief that had protected his head on a hot day and swinging it in circles to acknowledge the applause of the crowd as he ran among those who will always love him.

George Sheehan, MD, has crossed the final finish line. But the applause of the crowd continues.

Hal Higdon, senior writer for Runner's World *magazine, ran his first Boston Marathon in 1959 and was already an Old Hand when George Sheehan arrived there. Higdon wrote this column for the* South Bend Tribune.

C H A P T E R   1 7

LAST
INTERVIEWS

Ninety minutes and a world away from New York City lies an unlikely publishing center. Emmaus, a town of only a few thousand, is home to Rodale Press, which ships magazines and books by the millions. Rodale dominates this town but in a low-key, model-citizen way. You won't see any flashing neon signs boasting of Rodale's presence here, or any high-rise corporate headquarters. Rodale's operations are scattered about the town in more than a dozen renovated factories. One of these buildings houses *Runner's World* magazine.

George Sheehan is *RW's* best-known writer, and he lives only about two hours away on the Jersey Shore. Yet he seldom comes to Emmaus.

There's no need. He writes at home, then mails or faxes his columns for the *RW* editors to select and process. When George came here this summer, it wasn't on magazine business but to talk with the book editors. Rodale published his last two books (*Personal Best* and *Running to Win*) and wanted to bid on the next, which he still insisted on calling his "Death Book."

Runner's World editor Amby Burfoot had tried to arrange an interview since April, but George had resisted. For one who gets so personal in his writing and lecturing, he is curiously reluctant to be interviewed. He first told Burfoot, "You might catch me with my guard down."

He isn't shy, reclusive or ego-free. He simply has very high standards for his spoken and written words. He fears they'll disappoint his listeners, readers, or himself if he can't psych himself up as he does for a speech or self-edit as he does with a column. Burfoot persisted, though, and George agreed to sit for an interview (as he would do with several other reporters this summer) during the visit to Emmaus. They would talk into a tape recorder for an hour.

"He was clearly in the late stages of his seven-year battle with prostate cancer," Burfoot would write when this conversation appeared in the magazine. "Thin and drawn despite a blood transfusion the previous day, he needed help negotiating a flight of stairs and walked slowly, unsteadily, on his own.

"His deteriorating physical condition had taken no toll on his mind and spirit, however. As soon as we began the interview, I realized this was still the same energetic thinker and explorer we had known for so long. He seemed to relish each new question, particularly any that gave him a chance to talk about his latest project and obsession—the 'Death Book.'

"When I told George the hour was up, he looked surprised and checked his watch. I'm sure he could have gone another 10K."

Listen now to the Sheehan-Burfoot conversation.

§ § § §

You've run a lot of tough races in your life and always run them to the last gasp. Is this race against cancer the toughest?

No, there's nothing to this. It's no race. The challenge now is intellectual and emotional rather than physical.

But there is a similarity to running in the way I'm trying to deal with dying and write about it. The secret to my writing about running was always that I actually experienced everything I wrote about. I had inside information. I took running very seriously and writing about it very seriously. It's like what Thoreau said: There are no small subjects. You can take any subject and bring it to life through your own persona.

We runners, I think, are more or less born to run. Not everyone is born to run, but true runners are. And eventually we figure it out.

We are all, also, born to die eventually. And I believe we have to learn to pursue death and experience every-thing that happens to us along the way. That's what I'm doing now. I'm exploring the emotional, psychological, and spiritual challenges that are offered by the death experience. And I'm writing about them, just as I did about my running.

The method is identical. It's just that the two experi-ences are diametrically opposed. One is about reaching for peak performance, the other is about atrophy and oblivion.

You've said that at first you couldn't accept this dying experience. Now you have. What changed?

I'm no different from anybody else. When we learn about our cancer, we first try to bargain our way out of it. We say, "I'll be good from now on if only I can get off the hook and live longer." Then we start thinking about a cure. I went to Detroit, the National Institutes of Health, Sloan-Kettering... You name it, I went there.

And then finally I realized that no matter what they gave me, the chance for a cure was slim. So at that point I began to accept what was happening to me. And when you reach the stage of acceptance, that more or less puts you in command.

One of the things that has amazed me is that you were able to continue running and racing for so long.

I did that because I was addicted to racing. I can't believe how many races I've run in my life. Even with the cancer, I kept going as long as I could. At one point, I even quit the cancer treatments because I thought my racing was getting too slow. I had lost a minute a mile, so I stopped taking my medication. I wanted to be able to run faster, and I did. In 1989 I finished seventh in the World Veterans Championships in the 70–74 age group.

People thought I was out of my gourd to stop my shots just because my 5K times were getting too slow. But I was only thinking about the fact that I had lost a minute per mile, and I couldn't put up with that.

Besides, I always felt that I was an experiment of one, and no one had a history with a patient who stopped taking the cancer medication. No doctor would ever recommend it, and no patient would ever try it.

I figured I would be the one to try. And it turns out the

experiment worked.

What worked?

Stopping the shots that lowered my testosterone. As soon as I did that, my testosterone level came back up, and my muscle function improved. I may not have been as good as I would have been if I had never taken the medication, but I got down under thirty-six minutes for a five-miler.

Then the pain came, like a great white shark. I mean it was ferocious, and I could no longer go on without the medication.

Didn't you wonder that you might have been cutting your life short by going off the medication?

No. The history of these cancers is that there's always a point at which the medication no longer works. Everybody understands and accepts that. It's merely a question of time. How much time can the medication give you?

I knew that I would have a period of symptom-free living, but eventually the cancer would return. I never expected to get seven years. I've actually done very well. I have no regrets.

When I first found out about the cancer, I lay awake at night. I couldn't go to sleep. You really panic when you first get it. I was looking for solutions. I had domestic problems then and had had them for a period of time. But when the bad pain came, I made a complete reconciliation with the family. I went back [home], and it's been marvelous. Our family is so together since I got the cancer.

I never used to let anybody do anything for me. Now when I'm at home, they're always coming up and trying to do things for me. And we started having family gatherings every year. We've had four summer meetings that have been just great experiences for us. We sleep twelve and fifteen in one house, and gossip from six in the morning until late at night.

You've often called yourself an "underachiever"—that is, someone who's never really happy with the race he has just run or the speech given or the book written. Why do you suppose you're that way?

I don't know. Maybe the immigrant experience, siege mentality, Irish Catholic upbringing. My family never complimented me.

I never received praise for whatever I had done in school. I ran at Manhattan College, a big running school, but when I'd come into class after I'd won a big championship no one even knew it. I think I pursued life as a solitary, singular experience. And so my values were inside, not outside. I didn't look to anybody else for compliments. I went and did what I did the best I could do it. I was always the ultimate judge of what I achieved. Maybe I was a hard judge.

In just about everything I did—college, medical school, running, writing—I felt that I was just a cut below where I wanted to be. So I had to do everything I could to be the best.

You've written that running and racing are about self-discovery. What is the most important thing you've learned about yourself from all those years of racing?

Frequently it's an unconscious discovery, and you really don't know it has happened. You simply wake up one morning and realize something has been added to your life. I think we all have absolutely everything we need to be successful in our lives. But certain virtues don't come to us automatically. They're undeveloped.

When you enter a race, you don't finish it thinking that you have honed these virtues and now you're ready to become a successful person. But things do happen in races, and things come out of racing for reasons we're not sure of—things like justice, courage, and wisdom. And when you go out and race on a regular basis, you gradually come to embody these things.

But I'm asking you about yourself. *What's the most important thing* you *learned from running and racing?*

Let's see... I guess that I realized I was like most people, weak and sinful.

And that's the most important lesson?

Yes, because you have to have a starting point. You have to realize there are many things that you need to work on. I learned that I'd been doing a lot of things wrong. I wasn't so clever or smart or intelligent.

And I found philosophers who supported me in this. William James said that effort is the measure of a man, not talent.

Are any of the things that we learn through running appli-

cable outside of running? Can they make you a better person, or
can they only help you run a better race next month?

Well, I think that running a race is analogous to life. We
look at James Joyce's *Ulysses*, which boils down life's
odyssey to one day in Dublin. And we can think of a
marathon in the same way, that it makes all the demands
that an individual will face in an entire life. Actually, it
makes many demands that go unseen in an ordinary day.
It heightens and multiplies the demands, but the parallels
are still there.

Beyond that what we learn is that the most important
things are often the most ordinary and most implicit. We
learn from running that all we need to find is a basic
program that encourages things like exercise, a good
night's sleep, breakfast, not smoking, drinking in modera-
tion, and allowing maximum ability to do our thing,
whatever that is. I think running is a creative activity in a
sense. But I think the more important thing is that the athletic
experience has a counterpart in the aesthetic experience.

First you have the preparation. That's when you learn
where your heart is. Then you have the experience, and the
race becomes your art.

You've already made your body a work of art by training
to become an athlete. The race becomes your art because of
the challenge. When you come out the other side and
finish, you know you've been through this athletic and
aesthetic experience.

You've often said you couldn't write your books and columns
without running. What is it about running that releases some-
thing within you?

I always felt that way, but now that I can't run, I find that
I'm still able to write. But there's a difference.

The other night I was talking to one of my daughters,
and she noted that *Running & Being* was very different from
my more recent writing. She said it had a passion, an almost
juvenile enthusiasm. And I think that's probably true, because
every word of that book was written after running.

I had this pattern. I would write pages and pages of copy
that I called "mud," and then I would go out for a run. After
about thirty to thirty-five minutes, I'd go into overdrive. I'd
catch the third wind; that's when the ideas would start
coming like crazy. All I was trying to do at this point was
get the first sentence or first paragraph of the article

written. So I'd go home and write them up. If nothing else followed, I'd head out and start running again until the next ideas came.

Now I can't do any of this anymore. I can get on an exercise bike, but I don't get the same buzz from the bike. Then I lie down in bed, put my mind on the topic, and try to get the writing going.

I'm able to do this okay, but the words come out in a more mature tone because they're words recollected in tranquility. I haven't gone out and run. I haven't gone out and recreated the experience.

You've been called many nice things by many people—"guru," "poet," "philosopher." Which of these fits you best?
None of them. I like being called "George."

I hate guru because I think the Eastern religions struck out on it. They didn't believe in exercising, just meditation—a meditation to the point of near nothingness. So I'm no guru. But the media are such copycats that they all kept using the same word.

So it's George then. George, how would you like to be remembered?
I think I'd like to be just one of the gang. I'm not a star or anything. I've just had the good fortune to be in control of my time and to spend it on running and writing.

And then I also had the good fortune to be in the right place at the right time. Ten years after I got started, I just happened to be running down the middle of the road when all of a sudden there were millions of other runners out on the road with me. We raced against each other every weekend. And at some point, many years later, I learned something from all these races. I learned the ultimate truth about competition. I had been racing against the clock and racing against my opponents and racing against the weather and the hills and all of that. Finally I began racing against *myself*.

And when I did that, I learned what it means to become a runner. It means there's only one person in the race, and you're it.

E S S A Y

FINISH LINES

BY DICK PATRICK

Reading George Sheehan the columnist and hearing Sheehan the speaker should have prepared me for Sheehan the competitor. Still I was amazed at an indoor track meet in the mid-1980s.

The sixty-something Sheehan was running in a supposedly low-key celebrity relay. "Look out, here comes George!" shouted an official near the finish line.

No warning was necessary. Sheehan's legendary wheezing and moaning announced his arrival. Rounding the final turn out of control, he leaned for the finish and crashed to the boards, totally spent.

"Does it every year," said the official.

That is how Sheehan does everything—all out. He's now driving to complete another book and more of his columns that have numbered in the hundreds and influenced thousands. I visited him at home in New Jersey during what might be his final summer. George Sheehan, a pacesetter in the fitness movement for twenty-five years, now struggles on a flight of stairs. The former marathoner climbs by taking two steps per stair.

There is no more running or lecturing for Sheehan. "But I continue to write," he says.

By doing so, Sheehan is fulfilling one of his tenets. He is living the life he was meant to live.

"I think I was supposed to be a teacher, exploring and expressing ideas," he says. "And not merely teaching of the body but *through* the body. Physical education." His identity might be shifting. Sheehan says he's drifting to other topics, such as death and his family. "Getting cancer alerts you—I hate to use that expression 'wake-up call,' which is a cliche," Sheehan says. "Cancer has focused me to a finality. Suddenly I'm thinking about issues and personal situations that had been on the back burner."

Sheehan's columns can be intensely personal. He has

written about the pain of a relationship breaking up. In the 1980s he left his wife and family for six years before returning home. "What makes it more ridiculous," he says of his moving out, "was that I was sixty. [Joseph] Campbell talks of life being a labyrinth. There are a lot of blind alleys. I took some wrong turns."

The dedication to his 1989 book, *Personal Best*: "To Mary Jane and our sons and daughters, who waited with patience and love while I sought the light—and finally found my way home."

Sheehan now lives with his wife in their oceanfront home, a converted hotel with a dozen or so bedrooms, plus a porch drinking fountain for boardwalk runners. He's working on his eighth book, a personal account of the cancer plus a study of other philosophers' handling of death.

"I'm an experiential writer, and my available experience now is dying," he says. "I used to say it took three hours of running to produce a page of writing. Now it's three hours of dying... I suppose I shouldn't be so flip."

Irreverence is part of the Sheehan approach. So is hard, honest effort.

Sheehan measures success by effort. The memory of his diving for the finish is an appropriate metaphor for his life.

Dick Patrick writes for USA Today, *where parts of this piece first appeared in July 1993.*

CHAPTER 18

LAST LETTERS

George Sheehan's latest letter carried the postmark of this oceanside resort community. He was vacationing here with his wife, children, and their spouses and children. His work didn't stop during vacation. He wrote me two letters from Rehoboth Beach, and we exchanged a pair of phone calls. Mine were but a few of the contacts he made from here.

George works well on the road. He takes along no typewriter, and he doesn't own a laptop computer because he has never mastered computerese. His writing all starts with a pen and a yellow legal pad. The scrawl across these pages has "doctor" written all over it, but once you decode the words they're unmistakably Sheehan. He told of being at a beach house during the family's second vacation of the summer. He rested in one room. In another were "ten or so Sheehans in laughing conversation which I can vaguely hear."

"I see a huge votive candelabra. This is surely the way to go—the lights preceding me, praising the Lord. I am following a tradition that goes down through the centuries."

He wrote of his increasing weakness. He predicted that "today I will have one or two of my usual falls." Then he added, "But I know I'm on the right path."

George writes me letters like this every few days, and sometimes he mails several in separate envelopes the same day as inspiration strikes. He has written in airports, on planes, from hotel rooms all over the country and occasionally outside the U.S. borders. He fires these letters in all directions. This most direct and personal form of writing has touched thousands of people over the years, and it's another reason for the affection readers have for him. He has spoken to them this way—not as an anonymous fan in a crowd, but as a friend, one to one.

George sometimes laments that he never kept a journal. He hasn't needed one. He has left two distinct paper trails, his columns and his letters.

"I sometimes think of my columns as my journal, but I delude myself when I do," he has written. "These little essays can never be a substitute for a personal notebook. The column is too focused. The journal must include random thoughts. These should be everything from seedlings to fully fashioned truths."

His letters are his journal. Here lie his half-formed, hastily scrawled thoughts from which he fashions his essays. He seldom dates his letters to me. But their file folder says I received them in 1993, in roughly the order they appear here. They trace his thoughts and experiences through this year. One of the early letters from this file took note of how frankly he talked of his illness. "The truth is often blunt and to the point," he wrote. "Without my cancer my days would have sameness that I now wish to escape. Cancer is like everything else in life—an experience."

George has kept seeking new experiences this year. He signed up for a class in anthropology. He even considered flying to the Bahamas with daughter Monica to see the dolphins which are believed to possess mystical healing powers. He didn't make that trip and later quipped by letter, "Suppose I had been rejected by the dolphins. It would have been unbearable to be singled out as not fit for a man-dolphin relationship." His sense of humor remains healthy, as this and later letters show.

"There are times when the physical decline is humorous," he wrote. "I fell recently, next to my car in a small village. I couldn't get up. A woman saw me and thought I was fixing my car. My family, who knows I've never fixed anything, couldn't hold back their laughter."

In another letter he wrote that he "almost takes pleasure in doing battle. Some time ago I referred to myself as a mobile medical museum."

He told of a reporter challenging him last year about the ailments runners suffer in their supposedly health-giving sport. He let the reporter work through a long list of maladies and then ask again: Why put up with all this? George's answer: "It gives us bragging rights."

§ § § § §

Most of this year's letters have been serious. I wouldn't want you to think he's taking this fight lightly, so here is a more typical sampling of George's thoughts-by-mail. These letters usually contained, to use his description, "seedlings" of columns. But some came straight from his pen as "fully fashioned truths" boiled down to a paragraph or two:

> • The experiential writing on running, which has been my signature, has largely come to an end. My current fitness program consists of an occasional thirty-minute walk on the Boardwalk and ten to fifteen minutes on an exercise bike. Not much material there. I am through with running in the present, but I can use the past as illustration.

> • Fortunately there is a paper trail of weekly essays beginning in 1968, revealing an evolution of personality: slow, painful retreats as well as advances, marked by discovery of geniuses congenial with my genius. They confirmed my uniqueness, gave assent to my feeling of being different.

> • The man who comes down the mountain is not the same as the man who went up. The meaning is not as important as the experience itself.

> • Today I enrolled in an anthropology course. My cancer has liberated me for other pursuits. Otherwise I would keep to my schedule—weekdays and weekends following the usual progression. In the time I have left, I want to find different and interesting ways to live. Life is suddenly a pure sample of unfinished business. Here is where the urgency appears. How did I fail so much in living out my experiences?

• Attempting a cure [for his cancer] is the worst thing to do. All those therapies have side effects. We learn to live with cancer and at the same time obtain relief from pain. Otherwise we risk all the complications from medication—loss of hair, skin falling off, diarrhea, anemia, and other clinical conditions.

• I do not travel far from home these days. My cancer has shortened my day and limited the perimeter of my activities. Every week I turn down an invitation to travel and speak. I have regrets now about sights unseen, places not visited, friends scattered around this earth whom I'm unlikely to see again. I once said that most all my friends were a long-distance phone call away. They now have to be satisfied with my letters.

• Despite my situation of living in a restricted world, I am doing well. I plan the hegira for the day. Whom shall I have for a companion? What is the agenda? What will the day bring?

The point is not to give in.

• The lean surfer now needs someone to help him out of the ocean. I am learning the physics of getting out of bed, off the toilet, etc. As one who has finished twenty-one Boston Marathons, I am now going up stairs one step at a time.

• The writing has slowed to a trickle. The material is inside of me, but I can't get it out.

• The letters to you are a soliloquy that I hope will show us final form of my book. So I continue to write you. As I flesh out contents, it looks as if we will have to draw on other columns [besides those about his illness].

• Last time I used you to select the best columns, and the arrangements were up to me. I think your choices are better than mine, but my arrangements are better.

• I had a long visit with an editor about the two new books—the "Death Book" and the "Life Book." Unfortunately she is oblivious to the "Life Book" and concentrating on the "Death Book." She sees it as a major book. I promised it by the end of January 1994. We cannot let her dictate its timing and content unless it is the best way.

• I love the title "Final Instructions" [for the "Death Book"].

• Today I experienced the sudden onset of high-neck pain. My Percocet gave me some relief. However, two hours later I felt the return of a severe occipital headache. This may well be how I am to go. I am alone in the house on a weekend, when everyone could be available to bid me goodbye. And, God, I do feel as if this is the hour. I wonder how this time was selected—my book unfinished. I hope you will carry on the work.

• What last words do I have? Will they be, "How beautiful," or will they refer to the end of a perfect race? I wait for what comes next.

• I am disintegrating rapidly. I could use a wheelchair.

I am lost on which columns are my best and the arrangement, but you've done well in the past. You are my main man. Do your best.

§ § § § §

The do-your-best letter, written the first week of October 1993, would be my last from George. It wasn't simply a command to edit well on his behalf. It was a challenge to write and speak, run and live at my best.

He wasn't just speaking to me, of course. This has long been one of his bedrock themes: Do your best with what you're given. I relay his message to you now, along with a personal story that you might make your own.

Moving to a higher plane as a runner includes running marathons. I thought I'd retired from this event and pulled back to the distances that don't require two or three months of special training in advance and at least a month's recovery time afterward. My retirement from marathoning ended soon after George's began. We never discussed my taking the baton from him. He didn't ask me to do it, and I didn't put the idea into exactly these words until right now.

But his do-your-best admonition surely led back to this event. Running had gone somewhat flat without any challenge this large.

Amby Burfoot, George's and my boss at *Runner's World*, came out from Pennsylvania to watch the Portland

Marathon this fall. At dinner before the race he wondered, "What brought you back to running marathons?"

I told him the better question was who. Amby said, "Okay, then *who*?"

Several names came up, but none stood above George Sheehan's. I spoke of him again while telling an audience of runners on race eve, "Right now you're thinking only about yourself and what you have to do tomorrow. That's to be expected, because running the marathon is completely your responsibility.

"But with your training finished and your race not yet here, why not take a little time today to think about someone besides yourself? You aren't alone in this effort, you know. There's a 'who' behind each one of you. Someone inspired, encouraged, or challenged you to try a marathon. Someone taught you how to train, trained with you, or supported your extra training."

I urged these runners to think about who made their marathon possible, then to show their appreciation by dedicating the race to that person. They might run their race for someone who couldn't be there in person. They could do this graphically by printing a name on a shirt. I saw many signs like this on runners' shirts at the Portland Marathon.

Thoughtful as the gesture was, though, I didn't make it. My dedication was less formal but just as real. I didn't wear a name on my shirt but carried it in my heart. At Portland I ran for... no, make that ran *with* George Sheehan.

E S S A Y

HOME RUNS
BY ROBERT CULLINANE

There are no more runs for George Sheehan. No more mind-freeing jogs along the Jersey Shore.

The cancer has stolen his muscles. It has spotted his arms with sores and washed his face pale. And it has driven him to the aerie of his home in Ocean Grove, where he gazes out on the ocean and writes about life and death—both his and ours.

"I used to say that as a runner, it was my job to get injured and then to find out how to treat the injury," he says. "Now my job is to learn about how people die and to help them do it comfortably."

His own comfort now comes in the form of the two morphine pills he takes daily. Before the pills, "I felt terrible. I was going down the tubes. There were days I was in a fugue state." The morphine was an immediate blessing. But the lack of pain, Sheehan jokes, "is destroying the book. I'm feeling too good."

He starts to smile, but the "beep-beep-beep" of a monitor alarms us. He is having a blood transfusion as we speak, and the nurse runs over. She checks the life-giving tube attached to his arm. "It's just a clog," she reports.

"Great," says Sheehan. "I'll just sit here and explode."

His work these days is concentrated on his book. "It's given me new direction, new enthusiasm," he says. "It's enabled me to handle what's going on."

The book is about dying, what Sheehan often refers to as "closure." He says, "I feel uneasy sometimes. There's going to be closure. I never felt closure. Everything was always open-ended. Now everything that was on the back burner I'm bringing up."

And though he says dying is nothing like a race, he does consider it a sport—"a blood sport."

"It's a game that everyone is going to lose. Even the people who feel sorry for you are going to lose. They're just waiting their turn to get their fatal disease."

The nurse arrives with the lunch menu. "What's the soup du jour?" he grumbles. "Carrot and dill? Good God!" He orders Jell-O, custard, and ice cream. Then, almost as a comment on his diet, he says, "I've come to accept it." But he's talking about death again.

"I went through anger, the search for wonder drugs, the bargaining phase where you say, 'Let me live and I'll be a better person. Now I accept it. There are a lot of cancer patients who don't."

He considers himself something of a cameo actor in his own play. "Confrontation is not my way of dealing with this, not my way of doing things," he says. "My sister-in-law used to say, 'George faces his problems by turning his back on them.' I'm confronting death, but I'm doing it in a nonconfrontational style."

He thinks about immortality, too. "That's another thing dying people do. They think about what they can leave— their name on a building, or a family. I guess that's what this book is all about."

Then, as though reeling in his own ego, he says, "Somebody's going to pick this book up in some used bookstore fifteen years from now and say, 'Who is this guy? This is a really odd book.'"

His friend and fellow physician Dr. Richard Cohen says Sheehan "gets more out of life than most. He looks at what happens in his life as an opportunity."

His latest opportunity may be his most demanding.

"The Bible says that in his life, a man should plant a tree, build a house, write a book, and sire a son. I've done all that."

"You've built a house?" he's asked.

"I bought one. That counts."

And there's that smile again, breaking slowly beneath the pale blue eyes. He's ready to laugh, it seems. Ready to run off and laugh at the whole thing.

Robert Cullinane writes for the Asbury Park Press, *George Sheehan's local newspaper. He interviewed George in August 1993.*

CHAPTER 19

LAST CALLS

Cristina Negron, George Sheehan's and my editor at *Runner's World*, phoned from her office in Pennsylvania earlier this month. "Have you heard anything about George?" she asked.

She didn't say what the "anything" meant, but I knew from her voice that she brought bad news. I told her no, I'd heard nothing since George had called a few days before.

"Well, we just heard from Dick Patrick at *USA Today*. Someone who didn't identify himself had left a strange message on his voice-mail, saying that George had died."

Cristina was reluctant to call his New Jersey home herself and thought I'd be one of the first to hear. Not necessarily. If the worst had happened, dozens of Sheehans would need to be informed before anyone thought to notify me.

I had to call Ocean Grove right away. I hated doing it but couldn't stand not knowing.

My hand shook as I dialed the number. I expected to hear a distraught young Sheehan, an answering-machine message from George's wife Mary Jane, or a busy signal.

Instead a familiar voice came on the line and said, "Dr. Sheehan."

It was George himself.

Though I knew he'd lost most use of his legs and had to take drugs for his pain, he sounded good. I told him the day's upsetting story. He laughed and then invoked the words of Mark Twain: "Rumors of my demise have been greatly exaggerated."

True, but George is also aware that his time is short.

He has dealt productively, positively, and publicly with his cancer for seven years, and now it has advanced to its final stage. He has prepared himself for this stage, and now he's intent on softening the blow to everyone who loves and admires him.

"Walter Bortz called it right on the money," said George. His doctor friend from California had given him a treatment plan last spring that offered six more months, and they had been the good months promised.

"These six months have been a blessing," his son George added. "My mother has arranged frequent in-house dinner dates, inviting a few of his friends at a time. So he has had a chance to see people from his past—of all stripes—doctors, runners, friends, and relatives.

"As a family we've had two reunions. Both were terrific."

George's last months have been the subject of pre-obituaries in *USA Today*, *The New York Times*, *Sports Illustrated*, and several other publications. *Runner's World* is preparing, with his full knowledge and cooperation, a tribute section to appear soon after he dies.

He has upped his writing pace. His book is almost filled.

Those six good months are ending now. The blood transfusions aren't working their previous magic. George tells only as much about his condition as his listener wants to know. He says nothing about it unless asked, and he replies to direct questioning with the condensed version. I make a point of asking about his current health each time we talk. The day he squelched rumors of his own death, he said, "I'm having trouble swallowing. I'm only able to take liquids."

His slow, barely audible voice sounded more ominous than the words did.

§ § § § §

Almost two weeks passed with no more calls from George. He hadn't been silent that long all the years we've worked together, and this worried me. I feared he might not achieve two remaining goals, one minor and the other major. The first was to reach his seventy-fifth birthday, the second was to make final a publishing deal on his nearly complete book.

He's only thinking about the birthday, on November 5, as another reason for a family gathering. He has often said, "We are born with a seventy-year warranty," and he figures he has already outlived his own by almost half a decade.

The book was more worrisome. Random House had shown strong interest, but George himself was dragging his feet. This had nothing to do with his illness. It should have spurred him to move faster. But book negotiations have always gone slowly for George. His last deal (with Rodale Press, for *Running to Win*) took eight months between first discussion and signed contract. This one was moving at the same halting pace. Random House said it wanted the book. An editor made a verbal commitment to pay a five-figure advance that would be George's personal record.

Yet he hadn't yet committed in return. He wasn't sure he had enough essays, or which ones would and wouldn't go into the book, or in what order, or what to call this collection. I assured him repeatedly, as I had to do with each of his previous books, "The material is all here. You don't have to write another word unless you're willing and able."

He asked for and then rejected several of my sample chapter ideas. The first (and I still think best) was a simple, chronological, journal-like arrangement that started with his diagnosis in 1986. He wanted something more. He talked about a "personal evolution" and struggled to find an outline that matched his idea.

When he expressed frustration at finding none, I told him, "You could toss the columns into the air and let them fall in any order. They'd read just fine." We talked of titles. I'd suggested "Finish Lines," "Last Laps" and "Bell Lap." He turned them all down as too tied to running. My favorite, as noted earlier, was "Miles to Go." It never grabbed him.

George kept calling this the "Death Book," though he knew it wouldn't pass muster with the publisher. His other recent choices were "Going to Graceland"—named for the Paul Simon tape that that brings him comfort—and "Final Instructions."

He told me in the last phone call, "I can't deal with this book anymore. I'm counting on you to take over."

I said, "You've already handled it with the writing. "There are just two jobs left that only you can do."

The first was to tell me, in terms as general or specific as he wanted to make them, what he wanted the book to be. The second was to seal the deal.

He gave me a couple of unbendable rules on content. They were, "Use the columns as written, not revising or shortening them except to correct errors or eliminate duplication. And don't let anyone else add any commentary or tributes; let this be *my* book."

The deal appeared shaky. George hadn't reached any agreement with the Random House editors by mid-October, and he now sounded in no condition to talk any more business. But I knew, too, how George always approaches finish lines. Reaching them always takes guts, and he's throughly schooled in gutting out the hardest part.

"Guts is simply the decision to stand pain," he has written. "Some think guts is sprinting at the end of a race, but guts is what got you there to begin with.

"Guts start in the back hills, with six miles still to go and you're thinking of how you can get out of this race without anyone noticing. Guts begin when you still have forty minutes of torture left, and you're already hurting more than you can remember."

Young George called me to say, "We're set for the summit meeting. The editor, Kate Hartson, will come down here to the Shore on the 20th."

§ § § § §

I half-expected him to call back and tell me, "We had to cancel the meeting. Dad didn't feel up to it."

For the first time the illness has clouded George's mind. The greatest mind in running history—the one that had written at least a column a week for twenty-five years, that had dashed off a book every three years, that had stored the sayings of the world's great thinkers for instant recall when writing and speaking—is finding it hard to focus   on simple thoughts.

George III said, "He's still struggling to write, but it's only bits and pieces. I'm having a hard time seeing where they're going."

Dr. George may have written his last essay. But he wasn't finished working quite yet.

His last efforts have all been big ones. Isn't he, after all, the guy whose last race wasn't some rinky-dink fun-run but one of the country's biggest ten-milers? The guys whose last talk wasn't at a Kiwanis or Rotary luncheon in his hometown, but the Boston Marathon? His last published writing wasn't going to be a letter to the editor. It would be a book.

He once said, "At my age I could be retired. I could be sitting by the ocean, watching the waves roll in and out.

"But I feel I've never achieved all that I could. If you take less of a view than that, you're finished."

He had turned away from the ocean to push the book manuscript through to its end. Now he would make the publishing deal no matter how bad he felt. October 20 was one of his bad days physically, and he was indeed tempted to call off the meeting. But he had another promise to keep, one more finish line no matter how hard the final miles felt.

George III called me that day. "We're celebrating here in Ocean Grove," he said. Kate just left. She came to tell us that her boss had okayed the project and wants to call it *Going the Distance*. Here, I'll let you talk to the Big Guy."

George, Sr., came on the line. He had never sounded more tired.

"We're on," he told me. "Kate says we can give her the manuscript in any form we like, and then she'll ask for any adjustments needed.

"This will be up to you, Joe baby. I'm in deep trouble now."

Then came a pause so long I thought he'd dropped the phone or we had been cut off.

He finally added, "This has been my worst day and my best day." He sounded as exhausted yet ecstatic as a marathoner at race's ends. Now he could sit and watch the waves roll in and out. He could rest in the glorious peace that follows a big effort well made.

§ § § § §

Son George fills in details from recent weeks: "He isn't eating, and so far he has refused to be fed with a nose tube. His dietary treat is cracked ice. Jell-O and soft eggs are about all he can stomach."

Dr. George won't hear of checking into a hospital. The very word terrifies him, says young George. His dad knows all too well what happens to cancer patients inside hospitals, and he fears that once there he'll never come out.

"By early October he was getting extremely thin and weak—to the point where walking stairs was Heartbreak Hill," says his namesake. "We sensed that the finish line was within view. By mid-October he didn't have the strength even to use a walker. We moved a hospital bed into the family room, overlooking the ocean."

The family support has increased. His children now alternate taking days off from work so someone can always be in Ocean Grove during the week. "For the most part he is not in pain," says young George. "The morphine has seen to that.

"As he has weakened, we have to lift him from bed to chair. He has little feeling in those thin legs, so he has a child-like fear of falling and will cry out to us to be careful."

Son Andrew, the journalist, notices that "the pain has humbled him and sweetened him."

With the family he'd long decried sentimentality. Now, relates son George, "Dad frequently becomes teary-eyed with all his children. Nothing but praise for each one—each an individual 'experiment one,' as he said in his talks.

"For my mother he has said, 'These have been the best months of our lives.' Although he allows that when she becomes stingy with the pain-killers, 'Your mother is becoming like the dictatorial nurse in *One Flew Over the Cuckoo's Nest.*'"

Recently an Irish-born priest came to visit. Father James Brady talked privately with George that late afternoon. After this visit the priest took Mary Jane and George III aside. They found comfort in his words.

"Mary Jane," he said, "George is ready to go. He is at peace. He just wants the family to accept that."

E S S A Y
PARTING THOUGHTS
BY JIM MEMMOTT

George Sheehan—runner, doctor, writer, dying man—comes to the phone. At the other end of the line, I tell Sheehan that some of his fans in Rochester, New York, will be having a run in his honor in two weeks. Of late the cancer has hit hard. The Rochester runners want to do something before, not after, he dies.

Before I can explain this, Sheehan cuts in. He sounds like a man drifting in a dream. The morphine that dulls his pain may have left him confused. Perhaps he misunderstood the point of the call. Sheehan abruptly says he isn't as interested in cancer as he is in preventive medicine. He says he hopes to do something to help people change their lives and reduce their risk to disease. He seems to ramble.

I think of my father before he died. Sometimes he would include me in a phantom conversation when I walked in the room. After a minute I would take his hand and say, "How are you?"

With that question he would come out of his fog and look at me and smile and say, "Oh, Jimmy, I'm awful." Then we would talk.

Thinking of that, I ask Sheehan, "How are you?"

"Dreadful," he says. "Every week I'm reduced a little more." He speaks in that lucid, self-aware tone he used when he lectured.

"I'm like Longstreet. I'm backing off and hoping that the federalists are not going to attack."

This startling and perfect reference makes me blink. In the back of my mind, I remember Longstreet was a Confederate general at Gettysburg. I more or less recall that he was famous for his defensive stances.

Sheehan says his current book is coming along well. He is writing about death, the subject at hand. "I can get up to four hours to write," he says. "I enjoy the writing."

Sheehan says he now has to decide whether to submit to a different cancer treatment. "We had a family conference as to whether I wanted to go out there and fight," he says. "They come in and put a tube into you, and you fight that out. I'd rather just enjoy myself. I have tremendous days."

He describes a picture of himself in the arms of his grown sons at the beach. They are carrying him out to the water because he is so weak. Sheehan calls his sons "three enormous huskies." He says he is lucky to have such good children.

Then he says that he loves his wife, and he just enjoys being with her at their home on the New Jersey Shore. He is quiet. He may be crying.

I don't know what to say. I try to go back to the purpose of the call: the run honoring Sheehan. It will be a gentle gathering of good friends he may not have met. I don't get to tell Sheehan again about the run. Instead we finish our conversation as it began—talking about preventive medicine.

I realize that Sheehan may not have been in a dream when we began. Maybe—because his time is short—he was just in a hurry to say again and again that illnesses like his can be prevented.

Sheehan has learned this good message the hardest way, but he takes joy in the education. "The last three years have been wonderful," he says. "This has been a blessing to live through."

Jim Memmott of the Democrat and Chronicle *in Rochester, New York, published this essay—containing one of the last interviews with George Sheehan—on October 16, 1993.*

CHAPTER 20

LAST DAYS

George Sheehan admitted in a recent letter his fear that he might die alone. He needn't have worried.

The nearer he drew to his end, the more his family rallied around him. This might have been George's greatest accomplishment of his final years—bringing the family closer to him than it had ever been.

He had yielded much of the child-rearing to Mary Jane when the dozen Sheehans were young. George told Robert Cullinane in an *Asbury Park Press* interview this summer, "She raised the kids, and I worked and kept out of the way. I had two rules: Don't get on a motorcycle; and don't talk back to your mother."

George left home in the early 1980s and lived on his own for several years. But he said, "There wasn't a single day I was gone that I didn't think about going home."

He was home now. He would get his wish to die there, not in a hospital. His family would be there with him:

Mary Jane, who did such a marvelous job of raising these children that they stay this close as adults.

The twins named for their parents—George III, his dad's business manager, and Mary Jane, a mother of six.

Tim, a Port Authority of New York executive.

Ann, a psychologist.

Nora, a magazine art director.

Sarah, a special-education teacher.

Peter, a doctor.

Andrew, a TV news reporter.

John, a harness-race driver.

Stephen, a bartender.

Monica, an artist.

Michael, a securities trader.

Together they've given George and Mary Jane seventeen grandchildren to date. George joked this summer about the relatively modest count by Sheehan standards. "When my mother died she had seventy-six grandchildren and a total of 135 survivors. Somebody said it sounded like a plane crash."

§ § § § §

Young George Sheehan called a few minutes before nine the morning of November 1, a Monday. His greeting didn't hint of the news to follow.

We'd been talking every few days about his dad's final book and the deal they'd just made with Random House to publish it. They needed me back in New Jersey soon to talk about plans, and I thought this might be a call about travel arrangements.

He wasn't calling on business. His voice broke as he said, "Dad passed away this morning."

My first reaction was to say something meaningless. Then I asked how it had been at the end. He gave a few facts— George had died at 9:30 that morning, four days shy of his seventy-fifth birthday, with all his children there in the room looking out on the ocean—and promised details later. They arrived by letter shortly after the funeral. The oldest son wrote:

> The end came shortly after Father Brady spoke of Dad's acceptance of death. A bowel blockage caused by the morphine hardening the stool had Dad in real pain. Remedies included more painkillers.
>
> On the last Friday in October, he lapsed into a sleep which worked its way to Sunday night. A visiting nurse then told us he might die within twenty-four hours. That sleep was caused by the body breaking down, not the medication. Dad in a dark-blue turtleneck under the covers.
>
> At the very end a Willie Nelson tape was playing. He was singing his version of Paul Simon's "America's

Tune." Nelson shouted out the refrain, "It's all right, it's all right/We've lived so long so well."

Dad opened his eyes a moment. Then he fell back and died.

Some say life is not fair. Although his children were there at his bedside, Mom was not. This "domestic athlete," as Dad once wrote of her (to the chagrin of certain women), was out that morning running errands. While all of us were in tears around the bed, I noticed Mom parking her car in front of the house. No makeup man in Hollywood could have disguised our sorrow. But I said, "We can't let her know until she gets up to the living room."

I ran down and took her groceries. In front of me she began walking up the stairs. Her shrinking figure made me realize her age and how long they had been together, almost fifty years. When she reached the top and entered the kitchen, she saw the sad faces. And she knew.

She threw her hands up in front of her face, exclaiming, "Let me have him!" Then breaking through us, she ran to his bedside in the living room. Grabbing his head and smothering him with kisses, I heard her say, "I love you. We had a wonderful life."

A beautiful end. It's a story which still brings me to tears. I give it to you because stories of love should not be hidden.

§ § § §

Word of George's death spread quickly and widely. I received calls that day from as near to his home as Asbury Park, and as far away as Japan and Mexico. The news was reported on National Public Radio that day. Staff-written tributes appeared the next morning in two of the country's largest newspapers, *The New York Times* and *USA Today*, among many others.

A small sampling of the published praise:

> FRANK LITSKY, *New York Times*: "As a runner he was gaunt and ungainly and often successful. As a public speaker and author he was witty, self-deprecating and encouraging, with an unyielding zest for life."

> WAYNE LOCKWOOD, *San Diego Union-Tribune*: "It is gen-

erally agreed that the running movement in the U.S. was ignited by Frank Shorter's 1972 Olympic Marathon victory. But if it began with Shorter, it flourished under the eye and pen of Sheehan."

MICHAEL BEEBE, *Buffalo News*: "Before Sheehan we probably knew more about how our cars work than how our bodies do. He wasn't reckless or guilty of what some of his peers thought he was doing—practicing mail-order medicine. He was telling us that we ought to know what we are dealing with, that every ache and pain and twinge was not necessarily a threat to our running careers."

GIB TWYMAN, *Kansas City Star*: "I ran an hour today with George. Not in body but in spirit. In a way that would have been more meaningful to him. If it could be said that one man almost spiritualized running, that would be Sheehan."

MIKE TYMN, *Honolulu Advertiser*: "Until George began analyzing and writing about distance running, the sport was one of legs and lungs. He added heart and soul. He showed us that there is a vast metaphysical realm to what was widely thought to be nothing more than a mundane physical activity."

BRUCE BROTHERS, *St. Paul Pioneer Press*: "Thousands of runners at clinics from New York to Boston to San Francisco heard Sheehan deliver the gospel according to Everyman. He made you feel confident, joyous and worthwhile. George Sheehan was a believer, and he made believers of all who would listen."

MICHAEL HILL, *Baltimore Sun*: "A talk by Dr. Sheehan was the running community's equivalent of a Bruce Springsteen concert, though listening to him was more like taking off with John Coltrane on some improvised solo. Dr. Sheehan never used notes, and often paced back and forth nervously, gathering his thoughts and references before launching into that day's journey— taking his audience far afield before bringing them back to the original melody, which they now appreciated in a totally different way."

JOHN GRAHAM, *Best of Times*: "It is interesting that his talks were almost all compilations of other philosophers' ideas applied in a current formula. However, I think he will be remembered best for his own words."

MARK WINITZ, *RunCal*: "Although I didn't really know

George, like many runners I felt he was a close friend. Aren't we fortunate that he left so much of his wisdom?"

ELLIOTT DENMAN, *Asbury Park Press*: "Always The Doc had the best interests of his running friends at heart. A fixture on the front porch of the Sheehan home in Ocean Grove was a water fountain. Runners trotting by always knew where they'd find a cool sip on a hot day. The 'water station' will remain on the front porch as a fond reminder of him."

§ § § § §

"You meant a lot to him," young George said in his call on November 1.

"And I loved him deeply," I told him. He was like a second father, but more than that. George Sheehan was also my best male friend, the man I patterned myself after the most in work. He was—and is—my hero. We were back-to-back columnists in *Runner's World* from 1970 to the issue that came out the day he died. We worked together on books. We traveled the same speaking circuit. I'm a utility infielder, "a .230 hitter" as he sometimes called himself, in the Big Leagues. George is a Hall of Fame slugger.

But I never envied his fame. He always gave me someone to look up to and be inspired by.

I didn't cry over news of his death. Not at first, anyway. There would be time for that later.

First I had work to do. It started with a call to Amby Burfoot, the *Runner's World* editor. This activated the work he'd been planning for six months—and hoped he could hold off publishing indefinitely.

"I know it seems strange," Amby had told me last spring. "But we need to have a special tribute section on George ready when the time comes."

I'd written a past-tense column about him while he was still alive and working. Amby had taped an interview that George knew he would never see in print. "The time has come," I told Amby that Monday morning. By afternoon he called back to say, "We'll be running an eight-page insert in the January issue."

That magazine was already at the printer. But George had meant so much to the magazine's editors and readers that the eight pages would be a late addition to the regular issue.

Next I called John McGrath to say that time had come to run my tribute on George for *New England Runner* magazine and other regionals. John had asked me to write this piece a few weeks earlier and I'd finished it quickly, never figuring it would be needed so soon.

I wrote yet another version for my newsletter. This would combine with related material to form a special issue of *Running Commentary*, mailed on what would have been George's 75th birthday. His wake fell on that day, November 5. His funeral was the next day, a Saturday.

I didn't go back to New Jersey. This was my choice and the Sheehan family's.

Ann Sheehan phoned that week. "Have you talked to Mom?" she asked. I hadn't.

Mary Jane came on the line. Her husband had always called her "a saint." I'd call her "a rock." She has always been the family's foundation, the one who held all the Sheehans together while George was off being George.

She sounded as composed as ever. When I asked how she felt, Mary Jane said, "Very good. I almost feel guilty telling people that."

Her Catholic faith is unshakable. She believes that George has gone to a better place.

Mary Jane said what I was thinking: "We really think it would be better for you to come back here a few weeks from now.

"You can talk about his book then. Editing it will be the best memorial you can give him.

"Then we can all sit down and have dinner at the house. That wouldn't be possible with the crowds here this weekend."

I could picture the wake and funeral. I'm sure they were fitting tributes, with as many smiles as tears. I'm sure the crowds overflowed the school that George had cofounded and where his wake was held, and the Catholic church on his favorite race course. I'm sure the eulogies were many and were rich in memories. I'm sure his own written words were the backbones of the services.

I'll never hear his voice again. That slightly raspy, faintly New York–accented voice will never come over the phone again, as it did at least once a week for almost twenty-five years.

I won't have the voice. But I'll always have the words.

They're right here in my office with me. All seven of his books occupy a shelf of honor. Eight file folders holding his columns from as many years sit beside my desk, waiting to become his eighth book. Other essays and letter fills an entire file drawer behind me, and overflow into several cardboard boxes stored in the house.

We have enough material here for a ninth book and maybe a tenth. One will be a collection or his best lines, the other might be a fresh volume of his timeless advice.

George Sheehan is still at work. As long as his writing is read and he is remembered, he'll never be finished.

E s s a y

FOND FAREWELLS
BY JOE ADELIZZI

George Sheehan III couldn't help but smile as the crowd of well-wishers and followers of his father filtered into St. Michael's Roman Catholic Church for Dr. George Sheehan's funeral. They were coming in all shapes and sizes, wearing everything from Brooks Brothers suits to the sweats and sneakers that are as much a part of the running revolution as Dr. Sheehan's columns and advice.

"It seemed only right to have the funeral here," said George III. "It's right next door to Dad's favorite playground."

He was talking about Lake Takanassee, where runners are a more common sight than ducks. Dr. Sheehan wrote the book on running, which is why a bunch of runners were there at a packed St. Michael's.

Heck, even Fred Lebow, wearing his tribal clothing of sweatsuit, hat, and sneakers, was there to say goodbye. Lebow, the father of the New York City Marathon, was on his own deathbed three years earlier when a tumor on his brain was found to be malignant. Somehow he carried on.

Carrying on seems to be part of the running ethic. And no one carried on better than Dr. Sheehan.

The Rev. James Brady talked about death to those at the funeral. "Most of us hold death at an arm's length," said Brady. "Those with faith understand death as part of life, not something to fear but something to live with. George understood that death was a constant companion through the journey of life."

He understood that, and he took us places where we had never been before. Dr. Sheehan invited us into his mind for a journey toward death. Each week he documented for us his feelings, his needs, his desires.

The truth is, I hardly read a word of Dr. Sheehan's running columns back when he was talking about training and six-minute mile splits and what type of shoes to wear. The truth is, I couldn't miss a column when he began examining every fiber of his being as he prepared for death. Each column brought out another fear. Each time Dr. Sheehan battled through it. With every paragraph he was teaching a whole new bunch of readers—different from the runners and the like who had dubbed him the guru of that game. Now Dr. Sheehan was becoming the guru of life itself.

In his opening remarks Brady broke any tension in the room when he talked about the Sheehan family: "I want to extend my feelings to Mary Jane, and to George and Mary Jane, and Timothy and Ann and Nora, and Peter and Andrew and John and Stephen and Monica and Michael and Sarah... And isn't that a great Irish family?"

Laughter bounced from the aged church's walls by the time he was halfway through the list of Sheehan children.

"Three weeks ago I was with him," Brady recalled. "He said the last few months had been his best ever, because his wife Mary Jane and his children were all with him. He had the gift of being together."

"His final project was to die," said son Peter, also a doctor. "His other final project was to make his death easier for the family. He reunited the family that had been torn over the years.

Son Timothy added that Dr. Sheehan had instructed runners to start their races slowly and finish strongly. "This time he slowed and looked behind, and took my mother's hand, and my hand... and we crossed the finish line, fourteen abreast."

Brady talked about the professional side of George Sheehan, the doctor: "It was a tough time for him, giving up his practice. But he took to a new kind of healing. One of words and thoughts and deeds."

Joe Adelizzi is executive sports editor of the Asbury Park Press, *which published George Sheehan's columns for his last seven years. This article appeared in the* Press *the day after George's funeral.*

Epilogue

LASTING WORDS

Early in *Dr. Sheehan on Running*, his 1975 book, George explained his penchant for quoting the master thinkers of history—from Socrates to Santayana—in his own writing and speaking. "My family rarely gives me any credit for original thought," he wrote. "When a topic comes under discussion at the dinner table, someone is likely to turn to me and ask, 'What would Bucky Fuller say about that?'

"I am living proof that you can go through the world on borrowed words. Whatever happens, there seems to be someone who has already expressed my reaction to the event much better than I could.

"So I find it difficult to speak without giving voice to someone else's words. I quote them because they said so well what I was thinking. They described my experience, my personal truth, in miraculously right words."

In the process of becoming the best-loved writer and speaker in running, George himself became a valued source of quotable quotes. He gave voice to what other runners thought or felt or sensed, but couldn't find the words to express as well as he did.

Name any subject related to the running experience—and many subjects far removed from sports—and this master thinker had found just the right words to describe it. His friends and fans would ask ourselves, "What would George Sheehan say about that?"

When he died, I published the first special edition of my newsletter *Running Commentary* in its twelve-year history and devoted it entirely to him. George supplied more of the words than I did.

During an interview that last summer about his book, *Going the Distance*, he told Robert Lipsyte of *The New York Times*. "The book is going to be good. But the epilogue is going to be a problem."

My epilogue to this book about George Sheehan gave me no problem. All I needed to do was borrow his words from a talk he gave at the tribute dinner in April 1993. It's only right that the last words of this book be his.

The words survive. To a wordsmith that's the ultimate form of winning.

DID I WIN?
BY GEORGE SHEEHAN, MD

About one year ago, I was in a Unitarian church in San Diego, giving one of my sermons. There's no question I'm a preacher.

One of the questions was, "What is your big concern in life?" I turned to him like a child looking to heaven and said, "Did I win? Is this enough?"

It reminded me of Robert Frost when he was in his sixties. Somebody was talking to him about his view of life, how his life had gone, and he said he'd gone past good and evil.

He said, "What I'm concerned about is whether my offering will be acceptable." That's what you come to when you get into your sixties and seventies.

This weekend I was in Tyler, Texas, and one of my assignments was to speak at a Catholic school. I wondered what had I learned in seventy-four years that I could attempt to pass on to these youngsters?

One thing I've found over my years of talking is that you should never be concerned with what kind of performance you're putting on. What counts is what you can bring to the audience.

I brought the kids in Tyler the message that, fortunately, life is not a skill sport. Each one of us has everything we need to be a winner.

Runners learn this. It's very hard in the beginning to understand that the whole idea is not to beat the other runners. Eventually you learn that the competition is against the little voice inside you that wants you to quit. I told these kids that each one of them had the capability of being a winner, because winning is just triumphing over that little voice.

This transformation that occurs with running can occur in other activities. But the only way it can occur is through experience. You have to plunge into the experience. You have to make mistakes, go down blind alleys. There are no bad experiences; you learn from them all.

What we have going for us all the time are these experiences that we can be in and learn from. We can always be developing the virtues we need.

I was at one of the Boston Marathons when I saw an ad in the *Globe* for the Dana Farber Institute, a cancer center. The ad began, "Runners wanted."

"Runners wanted?" I thought. "They're not using mice anymore—they've become an endangered species?"

The ad went on to say, "We need people like you—people with energy, dedication, and discipline, and the feeling they can change things for the better."

You develop these capabilities through life experiences. You find, as runners seem to have found, those peak experiences that develop the self.

My son Andrew turned me on to this absolutely fabulous book called *All the Pretty Horses*. It's about a young man named John Grady Cole whose father is dying of cancer from smoking. On the last visit with his father, they go out on horseback.

The father is riding behind the seventeen-year-old boy, and he's thinking, "He rides that horse as if he was born on it. If he had been born in a country where there were no horses, he would have traveled until he found them, and he would have known that's where he was supposed to be."

It's the sureness about what he's doing and who he is that's so appealing in this story. You say to yourself, "Yes, horses were that to him. What should it be to me?" The only way I'm going to find out is through experience.

When I look around at my twelve children here tonight, it seems that every one of them is like John Grady Cole, riding in front of their father, doing what they were born to do. We all have to give our children the freedom and the education and the experience to come into that country where they were born to be.

Only then do you get beyond good and evil. You get to where your offering is acceptable.

I hope *Runner's World* doesn't find this out for awhile, but running is not my experience anymore. Dying is my current experience.

I'm going to take dying and elevate it. I am going to take it seriously, and I'm going to look at it and find out what it's all about.

Fortunately the first mate on this voyage is very logical and rational, well-disciplined, no nonsense. Mary Jane keeps things from going to pot. While I'm pursuing death in my own inimitable way, she's taking it very logically—really not being overwhelmed by it all. The other night we were sitting around and, apropos to nothing, she said, "Holy Spirit."

"Holy Spirit?" I asked.

"Yes," she said, "Holy Spirit. It's big enough, and they have a great choir."

Between the two of us, we're going to get this death thing really straightened out. It's going to be a great future.